The New Observer's Series

About the Book

The *Observer's* [...] annual pocket g[...] and helicopters, [...] lished aircraft typ[...] [...] ty third annual edition, embraces the latest fixed-wing and variable-geometry aeroplanes and rotorcraft of nineteen countries. Its scope ranges from such general aviation newcomers as the Gulfstream Peregrine, the Westwind Astra, the Reims-Cessna Caravan II, and the less conventional Beechcraft Starship and OMAC I, through the latest airliners, such as the ATR 42 which is likely to be one of the more noteworthy débutantes of 1984, to the newest military trainers as represented by the Skyfox, the AT-TC-3 and the IA 63. Provisional information is also included relating to the latest generation of Soviet military aircraft, such as Blackjack, Flanker, Foxhound, Fulcrum and Mainstay. The latest versions of a wide variety of established types are described and illustrated; all data has been checked and revised as necessary, and many of the three-view silhouettes depicting types appearing in previous editions have been revised to reflect the latest changes introduced by their manufacturers.

About the Author

William Green, compiler of the *Observer's Book of Aircraft* for 33 years, is internationally known for many works of aviation reference. William Green entered aviation journalism during the early years of World War II, subsequently serving with the RAF and resuming aviation writing in 1947. He is currently managing editor of one of the largest-circulation European-based aviation journals, *Air International*, and co-editor of *Air Enthusiast* and the *RAF Yearbook*.

The New Observer's Book of
Aircraft

Compiled by
William Green

with silhouettes by
Dennis Punnett

Describing 142 aircraft
with 247 illustrations

1984 edition

Frederick Warne

Copyright © Frederick Warne (Publishers) Ltd
London 1984

Thirty-third Edition 1984

Library of Congress Catalog
Card No 57 4425

ISBN 0 7232 1673 8

Printed in Great Britain by
Butler & Tanner Ltd, Frome and London

INTRODUCTION TO THE 1984 EDITION

The *Observer's Book of Aircraft*, for 1984—a year marking commencement of the ninth decade since Orville Wright initiated the saga of powered flight by staggering into the air at Kitty Hawk—embodies noteworthy contrasts. Not only does it see the return to its pages after many years of an aircraft of *biplane* configuration, albeit a modernised derivative of a type that first flew 36 years ago. It marks the return to the aviation scene of the canard—or tail-first—arrangement such as was considered logical by the Wright brothers for their "Flyer" of 80 years since!

The resurrection of foreplanes, as seen in the accompanying pages on the Avtek 400, the Beechcraft Starship and the OMAC I, is perhaps remarkable in that the obstetrics resulting in their rebirth have been performed for the benefit of the hitherto ultra conservative corporate executive transport market. Yet a further departure from the traditional is offered by another newcomer to the *Observer's Book*'s pages: the Grumman X-29A technology demonstrator. This not only embraces the once-again-fashionable foreplane, but signifies resuscitation of the swept-forward wing concept. However, these radical aircraft making their débuts in North American skies this year are, for the most part, noteworthy not *merely* for their unorthodox shapes, but for the advanced technology with which these shapes are mated.

The recession in the commercial air transport marketplace has continued. The past 12 months have seen termination of production of such as the TriStar and DC-10, the discontinuation of major new airliner programmes, the MD-90 and MD-100 being but two examples, and the dramatic cutting back in the production of other commerical transports. Nevertheless, this year will see a *fifth* new-generation regional airliner, the Franco-Italian ATR 42, join in flight test four competing aircraft that have all made their inaugural flights since publication of the last edition of the *Observer's Book*.

Insofar as military débutantes are concerned, 1984 appears likely to yield little, apart from the Italo-Brazilian AMX battle-field support aircraft and Argentina's IA 63 trainer. But in the following pages will be found provisional details—the emphasis being on *provisional*—of a new generation of Soviet military aircraft with such reporting names as *Blackjack*, *Flanker*, *Foxhound*, *Fulcrum* and *Mainstay*. If scarcely débutantes, having mostly been flying several years and near to IOC (Initial Operational Capability), these aircraft have not been included in previous editions as insufficient information has hitherto been available to permit publication of preliminary descriptions.

WILLIAM GREEN

AERITALIA-AERMACCHI-EMBRAER AMX

Countries of Origin: Italy and Brazil.
Type: Single-seat battlefield support and light attack aircraft.
Power Plant: One 11,030lb st (5 000 kgp) Rolls-Royce Spey Mk 807 turbofan.
Performance: (Estimated) Max speed, 720 mph (1 160 km/h) at 1,000 ft (305 m) or Mach 0·95; average cruise, 590 mph (950 km/h) at 2,000 ft (610 km/h) or Mach 0·77; combat radius (LO-LO-LO with 3,000 lb/1 360 kg ordnance and two 110 Imp gal/500 l drop tanks), 230 mls (370 km) including 5 min combat and 10 reserves, (HI-LO-LO-HI), 323 mls (520 km); ferry range (two 220 Imp gal/1 000 l drop tanks), 1,840 mls (2 965 km).
Weights: Operational empty, 14,330 lb (6 500 kg); max take-off, 25,353 lb (11 500 kg).
Armament: One (Italian) 20-mm M61A1 rotary cannon or two (Brazilian) 30-mm DEFA 553 cannon, two AIM-9L or similar AAMs at wingtips and max external load of 7,716 lb (3 500 kg) on five external hardpoints.
Status: First of six prototypes (fourth and sixth assembled in Brazil) expected to fly in July 1984, with anticipated peak production (combined Italian and Brazilian assembly lines) of 10 monthly against Italian and Brazilian requirements for 187 and 79 aircraft respectively.
Notes: The AMX is being developed by Aeritalia (47·1%) and Aermacchi (23·2%) of Italy, and Embraer (29·7%) of Brazil, with initial operational capability anticipated for 1987–88.

AERITALIA-AERMACCHI-EMBRAER AMX

Dimensions: Span, 29 ft 1½ in (8,87 m); length, 44 ft 6½ in (13,57 m); height, 15 ft 0¼ in (4,58 m); wing area, 226·05 sq ft (21,00 m²).

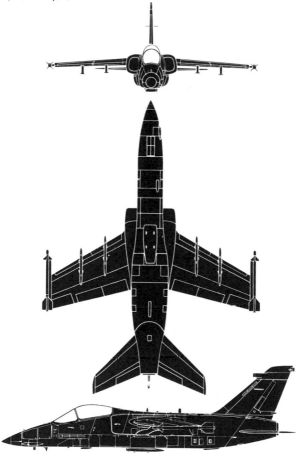

AERMACCHI MB-339A

Country of Origin: Italy.
Type: Tandem two-seat basic and advanced trainer.
Power Plant: One 4,000 lb st (1 814 kgp) Fiat-built Rolls-Royce Viper 632-43 or 4,580 lb st (2 077 kgp) Viper 680–43 turbojet.
Performance: (Viper 632-43) Max speed, 558 mph (898 km/h) at sea level, 508 mph (817 km/h) at 30,000 ft (9 145 m); initial climb, 6,195 ft/min (33,5 m/sec); service ceiling, 48,-000 ft (14 630 m); max range (internal fuel with 10% reserves), 1,093 mls (1 760 km).
Weights: Empty, 6,780 lb (3 075) kg); normal loaded, 9,700 lb (4 400 kg); max take-off, 13,000 lb (5 897 kg).
Armament: (Training and light strike) Up to 4,000 lb (1 815 kg) of ordnance between six underwing stations.
Status: First of two prototypes flown 12 August 1976, with deliveries to Italian Air Force commencing February 1981, these being preceded by first export deliveries (10 for Argentine Navy) commencing November 1980. Orders for Italian Air Force totalled 81 by beginning of 1984, export orders including 12 for Malaysia, 12 for Nigeria and 16 for Peru. Last-mentioned country is to assemble a further 50 under licence in a pro-gramme by Indaer-Macchi to culminate in indigenous manu-facture of wings, rear fuselage and tail assembly. Production rate is currently three monthly.
Notes: The uprated Viper 680-43 entered flight test in the MB-339A late June 1983, and production aircraft with this engine will be available during 1984. This engine is also being proposed for the single-seat light close air support version, the MB-339K Veltro 2 (see 1981 edition) which is to be fitted with a head-up display and an inertial nav/attack system during 1984. The 100th production MB-339 was completed mid-May 1983.

AERMACCHI MB-339A

Dimensions: Span, 35 ft 7 in (10,86 m); length, 36 ft 0 in (10,97 m); height, 13 ft 1 in (3,99 m); wing area, 207·74 sq ft (19,30 m²).

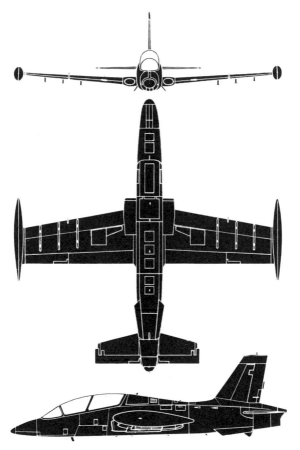

AÉROSPATIALE TB 30 EPSILON

Country of Origin: France.
Type: Tandem two-seat primary/basic trainer.
Power Plant: One 300 hp Avco Lycoming AEIO-540-LIB5-D six-cylinder horizontally-opposed engine.
Performance: Max speed, 235 mph (378 km/h) at sea level; cruise (75% power), 225 mph (363 km/h) at 6,000 ft (1 830 m); max initial climb, 1,850 ft/min (9,4 m/sec); service ceiling, 22,965 ft (7 000 m); endurance (75% power), 3·75 hrs.
Weights: Empty equipped, 1,936 lb (878 kg); max take-off, 2,755 lb (1 250 kg).
Status: Two prototypes flown on 22 December 1979 and 12 July 1980 respectively, and first production aircraft flown on 29 June 1983. Total of 60 ordered by beginning of 1984 against total *Armée de l'Air* requirement for 150 aircraft, with four delivered during 1983 and production tempo of three monthly to be attained during course of 1984.
Notes: The Epsilon, designed to simulate some of the flying characteristics of more advanced jet aircraft (eg. spinning and stalling) is scheduled to enter *Armée de l'Air* service from October 1984, when the first instructional course will commence at Cognac. Students will fly 70 hours on the Epsilon (rather than the present 26 hours on the CAP 10 and 64 hours on the turbojet-powered Magister) during the initial training phase, the long-term aim being to eliminate the subsequent 60-hour Magister stage and replace it with a further 80-hour Epsilon stage. A proposed export version will embody four wing hardpoints for up to 578 lb (262 kg) of ordnance for weapons training and light attack tasks. Consideration was being given at the beginning of 1984 to development of a turboprop-powered version with an Allison 250-C engine.

AEROSPATIALE TB 30 EPSILON

Dimensions: Span, 25 ft 11½ in (7,92 m); length, 24 ft 10½ in (7,59 m); height, 8 ft 8¾ in (2,66 m); wing area, 103·34 sq ft (9,60 m²).

AÉROSPATIALE-AERITALIA ATR 42

Countries of Origin: France and Italy.
Type: Regional airliner.
Power Plant: Two 1,800 shp Pratt & Whitney (Canada) PW120 turboprops.
Performance: (ATR 42-100) Max cruise speed, 317 mph (511 km/h) at 20,000 ft (6 095 m); max initial climb, 1,860 ft/min (9,45 m/sec); cruise ceiling, 25,000 ft (7 620 m); max range (with 42 passengers and reserves), 838 mls (1 350 km) at econ cruise at 25,000 ft (7 620 m).
Weights: Operational empty (-100), 20,900 lb (9 480 kg), (-200), 21,184 lb (9 609 kg); max take-off (-100), 32,850 lb (14 900 kg), (-200), 34,720 lb (15 750 kg).
Accommodation: Flight crew of two and four-abreast seating for (-100) 42 or (-200) 46 or 50 passengers with central aisle.
Status: Prototype scheduled to enter flight test in August 1984, with second and third (pre-series aircraft following in October–November 1984 and April 1985, certification being planned for September 1985. Current planning anticipates completion of five series aircraft in 1985 and 33 in 1986, a production rate of four monthly being attained by early 1987. Forty-seven had been ordered by the beginning of 1984, with a further 16 on option. The first ATR 42 is expected to be delivered to Air Littoral in France by September 1985.
Notes: The ATR (*Avion de Transport Régional*) 42 is being developed jointly by Aérospatiale of France and Aeritalia of Italy on a 50-50 basis. The former is responsible for the wing, the horizontal tail surfaces and rudder, the engine nacelles, instrumentation, avionics and final asssembly, the latter producing the complete fuselage, the tail fin, the primary cockpit structure, the undercarriage, the flight controls and various systems.

AÉROSPATIALE-AERITALIA ATR 42

Dimensions: Span, 80 ft 7⅓ in (24,57 m); length, 74 ft 5¾ in (22,70 m); height, 24 ft 10⅝ in (7,59 m); wing area, 586·65 sq ft (54,50 m²).

AIDC AT-TC-3

Country of Origin: Taiwan (Formosa).
Type: Tandem two-seat basic/advanced trainer.
Power Plant: Two 3,500 lb st (1 588 kgp) Garrett TFE 731-2-2L turbofans.
Performance: Max speed, 558 mph (898 km/h) at sea level, 560 mph (900 km/h) or Mach 0·85 at 36,000 ft (10 975 m); initial climb, 8,000 ft/min (40,7 m/sec); service ceiling, 48,000 ft (14 625 m); endurance (max internal fuel), 3·2 hrs.
Weights: Empty equipped, 8,500 lb (3 855 kg); normal loaded (training mission), 11,500 lb (7 485 kg); max take-off (weapons training and light strike), 16,500 lb (7 485 kg).
Armament: Provision for AIM-9 Sidewinder AAM at each wing tip, internal bay beneath rear cockpit for various ordnance, including semi-recessed machine gun pack, and hardpoints on fuselage centreline and beneath each wing for practice bombs, missiles and other stores.
Status: Two prototypes (XAT-3s) flown on 16 September 1980 and 31 October 1981 respectively. Series production (as AT-TC-3) for the Chinese Nationalist Air Force initiated in March 1982.
Notes: Manufactured by the Aero Industry Development Centre and scheduled to enter service with the CNAF during the course of 1984, the AT-TC-3 was developed under a contract awarded in July 1975 in collaboration with Northrop. While primarily intended for the training role, the AT-TC-3 has a secondary light attack role and is unusual among aircraft in its category in having an internal weapons bay. This can accommodate quick-change weapons packs, bombs or a variety of other stores. Provision is made for wingtip-mounted missiles for self defence and emergency air defence. The CNAF reportedly has a requirement for 50 aircraft of this type for the flying and weapons training roles.

AIDC AT-TC-3

Dimensions: Span, 34 ft 4 in (10,46 m); length (including nose probe), 42 ft 4 in (12,90 m); height, 14 ft 3½ in (4,36 m); wing area, 236·06 sq ft (21,93 m²).

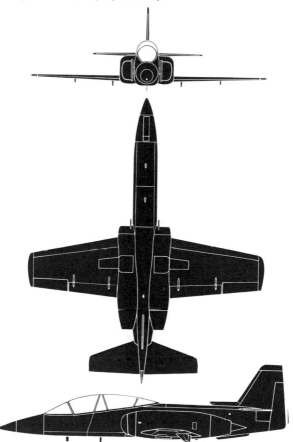

AIRBUS A300-600

Country of Origin: International consortium.

Type: Medium-haul commercial airliner.

Power Plant: Two 56,000 lb st (25 400 kgp) Pratt & Whitney JT9D-7R4H1 or General Electric CF6-80C2 turbofans.

Performance: Max cruise speed, 554 mph (891 km/h) at 31,000 ft (9 450 m); econ cruise, 536 mph (862 km/h) at 33,000 ft (10 060 m); range cruise, 518 mph (833 km/h) at 35,000 ft (10 670 m); range (max payload), 3,430 mls (5 200 km) at econ cruise, (max fuel with 52,900-lb/23 995-kg payload), 5,320 mls (8 560 km).

Weights: Operational empty, 193,410 lb (87 728 kg); max take-off, 363,760 lb (165,000 kg).

Accommodation: Flight crew of three and maximum seating for 344 passengers, a typical arrangement being for 267 passengers in a mixed-class layout.

Status: First A300-600 flown on 8 July 1983, with second flown November 1983, and third scheduled to have flown in February 1984. Certification was planned for mid-March 1984, with first customer delivery (to Saudia) following in May. Total of 244 A300s (all versions) ordered by beginning of 1984 when more than 220 had been delivered. Production rate (including A310) being reduced from five to three monthly at beginning of 1984.

Notes: The A300 is manufactured by a consortium of Aérospatiale (France), British Aerospace (UK), Deutsche Airbus (Federal Germany) and CASA (Spain). The latest version, the A300-600, replaces the A300B4-200 (see 1983 edition) from which if differs primarily in having the new, re-profiled rear fuselage of the A310 with an extension of the parallel portion of the fuselage offering an 18-seat increase in passenger capacity, and later-generation engines as offered with the A310. The first CF6-80C2-powered -600 will fly in March 1985, and delivery will be made to Thai International after certification in the following September.

AIRBUS A300-600

Dimensions: Span, 147 ft 1¼ in (44,84 m); length, 177 ft 5 in (54,08 m); height, 54 ft 3 in (16,53 m); wing area, 2,799 sq ft (260,00 m²).

AIRBUS A310-200

Country of Origin: International consortium.

Type: Short/medium-haul commercial airliner.

Power Plant: Two 48,000 lb st (21 800 kgp) General Electric CF6-80A1 or Pratt & Whitney JT9D-7R4D1, or 50,000 lb st (22 680 kgp) CF6-80A3 or JT9D-7R4E1 turbofans.

Performance: Max cruise speed, 562 mph (904 km/h) at 33,000 ft (10 060 m); econ. cruise, 528 mph (850 km/h) at 37,000 ft (11 280 m); long-range cruise, 522 mph (840 km/h) at 39,000 ft (11 885 m); range (236 passengers), 2,995 mls (4 820 km), (max. payload), 1,440 mls (2 315 km).

Weights: Operational empty (typical), 175,863 lb (79 770 kg); max take-off, 291,010 lb (132 000 kg), (option), 305,560 lb (138 600 kg).

Accommodation: Flight crew of two or three with single-class seating for 236 or 262 passengers eight abreast, or (typical mixed-class) 20 first-class six-abreast and 200 economy-class eight abreast.

Status: First A310 flown on 3 April 1982, with first customer delivery (to Swissair) spring 1983. Total of 108 A310s ordered by beginning of 1984, when production rate (including A300—see pages 16–17) was being reduced from five to three monthly, with some 20 delivered.

Notes: By comparison with the earlier A300B, the A310 has a new, higher aspect ratio wing, a shorter fuselage, a new, smaller tailplane and a new undercarriage, but retains a high degree of commonality with the preceding and larger aircraft. Like the A300B, the A310 is being built by a consortium of French, British, Federal German and Spanish companies, with Belgian (SONACA) and Dutch (Fokker) companies being associated with the programme. The longer-range A310-300 (ordered by Swissair) will be delivered from late 1985, having an effective range (with 218 passengers) of 4,605 mls (7 410 km).

AIRBUS A310-200

Dimensions: Span, 144 ft 0 in (43,90 m); length, 153 ft 1 in (46,66 m); height, 51 ft 10 in (15,81 m); wing area, 2,357·3 sq ft (219,00 m²).

ANTONOV AN-3

Country of Origin: USSR.
Type: Light utility transport and agricultural aircraft.
Power Plant: One 1,450 shp Glushenkov TVD-20 turboprop.
Performance: Normal cruise speed, 112 mph (180 km/h). No further details available.
Weights: Max take-off, 12,787 lb (5 800 kg).
Accommodation: Crew of two on flight deck and up to 12 passengers in main cabin.
Status: The An-3 has been under development by the Antonov bureau for a number of years and prototypes powered by the earlier TVD-10 turboprop are known to have been flying in the late 'seventies.
Notes: The An-3 utility biplane has been developed from the piston-engined An-2 which was first flown on 31 August 1947 and of which more than 5,000 were built in the Soviet Union before production was transferred to the WSK-Mielec in Poland where more than 9,000 were subsequently built. The An-3 is intended to succeed the An-2 in the agricultural and utility roles in Comecon countries and production is to be undertaken at the WSK-Mielec. Apart from some systems modernisation, the An-3 is essentially similar to its predecessor, but associated with the introduction of the turboprop engine (which is lighter than the piston engine that it supplants) is a lengthening of the forward fuselage by means of a plug between the wings and the cockpit. In all other respects, the An-3 is apparently structurally similar to the An-2. The An-3 is suitable for both spraying and dusting, the cockpit being sealed to protect the crew from insecticide and features air conditioning for use when the aircraft is operating in high ambient conditions such as are frequently encountered at low altitudes.

ANTONOV AN-3

Dimensions: Span, 59 ft 8½ in (18,18 m); length (approx), 47 ft 0 in (14,33 m); height, 13 ft 1½ in (4,00 m); wing area, 770 sq ft (71,6 m²).

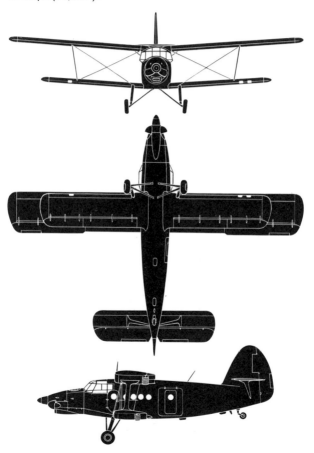

ANTONOV AN-28 (CASH)

Country of Origin: USSR.

Type: Light STOL utility transport.

Power Plant: Two 960 shp PZL-Rzeszov-built Glushenkov PZL-10S (TVD-10B) turboprops.

Performance: Max cruise speed, 217 mph (350 km/h); econ cruise, 186 mph (300 km/h); max initial climb, 2,460 ft/min (12,49 m/sec); range (with max fuel), 807 mls (1 300 km) at econ cruise, (with 15 passengers), 410 mls (660 km), (with 18 passengers), 233 mls (375 km).

Weights: Empty, 8,267 lb (3 750 kg); normal loaded, 12,785 lb (5 800 kg); max take-off, 14,330 lb (6 500 kg).

Accommodation: Flight crew of one or two and basic arrangement (light regional transport role) for 15 seats three abreast with offset aisle, or up to 20 seats in high-density configuration. An aeromedical version can accommodate six casualty stretchers, five seated casualties and a medical attendant. An electrically-actuated rear ramp facilitates straight-through loading for the freighter role.

Status: Initial prototype flown (as An-14M) in September 1969, with production prototype following early in 1974. Further pre-series aircraft produced in Soviet Union before entire programme transferred to Poland where first production examples completed in last quarter of 1983, with first deliveries of feederliner version (to Aeroflot) scheduled for mid-1984.

Notes: Manufacture of the An-28 is now being undertaken under licence by PZL at Mielec, current planning calling for the export of 1,200 aircraft of this type to the Soviet Union by 1990, with an annual production rate of the order of 200 aircraft. A substantial proportion of the An-28s to be built will fulfil the agricultural role.

ANTONOV AN-28 (CASH)

Dimensions: Span, 72 ft 2⅛ in (22,06 m); length, 42 ft 6⅞ in (12,98 m); height, 15 ft 1 in (4,60 m); wing area, 433·58 sq ft (40,28 m²).

ANTONOV AN-32 (CLINE)

Country of Origin: USSR.
Type: Military tactical transport.
Power Plant: Two 4,190 ehp Ivchenko AI-20M or 5,112 ehp AI-20DM turboprops.
Performance: (AI-20M) Max continuous cruise speed, 317 mph (510 km/h) at 26,250 ft (8 000 m); service ceiling, 31,150 ft (9 500 m); range (max payload and 45 min reserve), 497 mls (800 km), (max fuel), 1,367 mls (2 200 km).
Weights: Max take-off, 57,270 lb (26 000 kg).
Accommodation: Flight crew of five and 39 troops on tip-up seats along fuselage sides, 30 fully-equipped paratroops or 24 casualty stretchers and one medical attendant. A maximum of 13,227 lb (6 000 kg) of freight may be carried, loading being facilitated by a rear ramp and a 4,409-lb (2 000-kg) capacity cargo hoist.
Status: The prototype An-32 was flown late 1976, and production initiated 1981 against an order for 95 aircraft from the Indian Air Force. Pre-series aircraft flown late 1982, and deliveries to India scheduled to commence late 1983/early 1984. Other customers include Tanzania and Cape Verde.
Notes: Based on the airframe of the An-26 (Curl), but embodying structural strengthening to absorb a one-third increase in installed power, the An-32 was developed specifically to meet a requirement formulated by the Indian Air Force for a medium tactical transport possessing good "hot-and-high" performance characteristics coupled with good field performance and the ability to operate from unpaved strips with minimal support. The AI-20DM-powered An-32 is expected to enter Indian service in the first half of 1984 as a successor to the Fairchild C-119. A variety of small wheeled or tracked vehicles can be accommodated.

ANTONOV AN-32 (CLINE)

Dimensions: Span, 95 ft 9½ in (29,20 m); length, 78 ft 1 in (23,80 m); height, 28 ft 1½ in (8,58 m); wing area, 807·1 sq ft (74,98 m²).

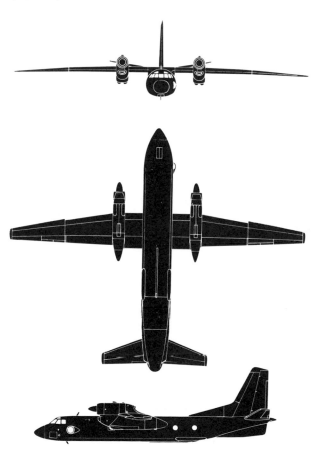

AVTEK 400

Country of Origin: USA.

Type: Light corporate transport.

Power Plant: Two 680 shp Pratt & Whitney (Canada) PT6A-28 turboprops.

Performance: (Estimated) Max speed, 425 mph (684 km/h); initial climb, 5,400 ft/min (27,4 m/sec); service ceiling, 37,000 ft (11 280 m); range (with full payload), 2,600 mls (4 185 km).

Weights: Max take-off, 5,500 lb (2 495 kg).

Accommodation: Pilot and co-pilot/passenger on flight deck and seating for four-seven passengers in manin cabin.

Status: The prototype Avtek 400 was scheduled to commence flight trials early in 1984, with certification anticipated early 1985. Advance planning calls for production of 100 aircraft in 1985 followed by 160 in 1986.

Notes: Of highly unconventional configuration, the Avtek 400 is constructed almost totally of Du Pont Kevlar aramid fibre composite skins with a Nomex honeycomb filling, graphite reinforcement being used with the aramid fibre material where high compressive strength is required (eg, the wing spars). The Avtek 400 is thus likely to be one of the first light corporate executive transports manufactured primarily of composite materials to attain production, the first being the Lear Fan 2100 (see pages 128–129). Claimed to weigh little more than half of its similarly-sized contemporaries manufactured from conventional materials, the Avtek 400 is expected to be assembled by Aeronca Inc from components supplied by Japanese subcontractors experienced in handling composites.

AVTEK 400

Dimensions: Span, 34 ft 0 in (10,36 m); length, 34 ft 0 in (10,36 m); height, 10 ft 1 in (3,07 m).

BEECHCRAFT 1900

Country of Origin: USA.

Type: Regional airliner and corporate transport.

Power Plant: Two 1,100 shp Pratt & Whitney (Canada) PT6A-65B tuuboprops.

Performance: Max cruising speed, 303 mph (488 km/h) at 10,000 ft (3 050 m); long-range cruise, 250 mph (402 km/h) at 10,000 ft (3 050 m); initial climb, 2,280 ft/min (11,6 m/sec); service ceiling, 25,000 ft (7 620 m); max range (19 passengers at cost econ cruise), 639 mls (1 028 km) at 10,000 ft (3 050 m), 977 mls (1 572 km) at 25,000 ft (7 620 m).

Weights: Operational empty (standard), 8,500 lb (3 856 kg); max. take-off, 16,600 lb (7 530 kg).

Accommodation: Flight crew of two and 19 passengers two-abreast with central aisle, with optional arrangement for 16 passengers two-abreast plus three abreast at cabin rear. Corporate transport version currently on offer has typical seating for eight to fourteen passengers, the latter having six in forward cabin and eight in aft cabin.

Status: First of three prototypes flown on 3 September 1982, with certification following in 22 November 1983, at which time first customer delivery was scheduled. Production rate of four monthly expected to be attained in August 1984.

Notes: The Beechcraft 1900 has been derived from the Super King Air, with which there is approximately 40 per cent commonality of component parts. Tail-lets projecting beneath the tailplane and stabilons on the rear fuselage improve directional and pitch stability. The Beechcraft 1900 is available with a cargo door option.

BEECHCRAFT 1900

Dimensions: Span, 54 ft 6 in (16,61 m); length, 57 ft 10 in (17,63 m); height, 14 ft 10¾ in (4,53 m); wing area, 303 sq ft (28,15 m²).

BEECHCRAFT LIGHTNING 38P

Country of Origin: USA.
Type: Light cabin monoplane.
Power Plant: One 650 shp Pratt & Whitney (Canada) PT6A-40 turboprop.
Performance: Max cruise speed, 323 mph (520 km/h) at 25,000 ft (7 620 m); range (at max power cruise with 45 min reserves), 1,075 mls (1 730 km); max range, 1,381 mls (2 222 km) at 242 mph (389 km/h).
Weights: Typical max take-off, 5,800 lb (2 631 kg).
Accommodation: Four individual seats in pairs with optional fifth and sixth seats.
Status: Engineering test-bed (PD-336) flown on 14 June 1982. The first of two flying prototypes (EJ-1 and EJ-2) was scheduled to enter flight test in December 1983, and certification is to be completed during 1984, with customer deliveries commencing immediately thereafter.
Notes: Based on the wing and fuselage structure of the twin-engined pressurised Baron 58P, the Lightning is to be offered with three alternative engines. The engineering test-bed (Preliminary Design 336) is powered by a 650 shp flat-rated Garrett TPE331-9, this being illustrated above and right, and the first prototype (EJ-1) to be used for certification is powered by a PT6A-40. A subsequent aircraft will be fitted with the 650 shp flat-rated PT6A-116. The data quoted above is provisional and is based on the flight testing of the PD-336, and Beech Aircraft held 80 letters of intent for the Lightning by October 1983. Apart from engine, the production prototype will differ from the engineering test bed in having a new exhaust system which will pipe the gases along each side of the engine.

BEECHCRAFT LIGHTNING 38P

Dimensions: Span, 37 ft 10 in (11,53 m); length, 30 ft 0 in (9,14 m); height, 9 ft 0 in (2,74 m), wing area, 188.1 sq ft (17,48 m²).

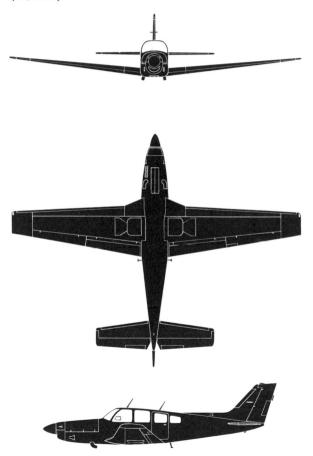

BEECHCRAFT STARSHIP 1

Country of Origin: USA.

Type: Light corporate executive transport.

Power Plant: Two 1,000 shp Pratt & Whitney (Canada) PT6A-60 turboprops.

Performance: (Estimated) Max cruising speed, 400 mph (644 km/h) at 41,000 ft (12 495 m); max climb, 3,300 ft/min (16,76 m/sec); range (with 45 min reserves), 2,070 mls (3 330 km).

Weights: Loaded, 12,500 lb (5 670 kg).

Accommodation: Pilot and co-pilot on flight deck and eight-ten passengers in main cabin with six basic interior configurations. A typical cabin will have a four-seat forward club section with seating for three more passengers on an aft seat facing a two-place divan.

Status: An 85 per cent scale version of the Starship was flown on 29 August 1983, with four full-scale flight test aircraft and two ground test aircraft two be built for certification during 1985.

Notes: The Starship is of innovative concept in that it is of canard configuration, the foreplane being capable of variable sweep angle and extensive use being made of composite materials in the construction of the aircraft. The 85 per cent scale version (illustrated above) was developed and built for the Beech Aircraft Corporation by Scaled Composites Inc, and the configuration of the Starship is based on that of the Rutan VariEze light plane which has been built by amateurs.

BEECHCRAFT STARSHIP 1

Dimensions: Span, 54 ft 7 in (16,64 m); length, 45 ft 5 in (13,84 m).

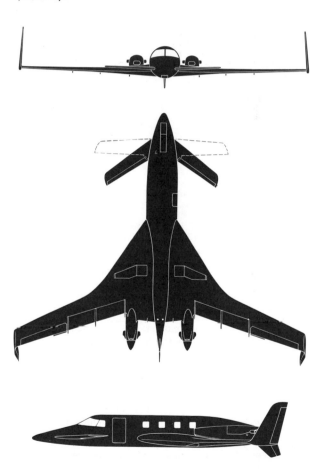

BEECHCRAFT T-34C (TURBINE MENTOR)

Country of Origin: USA.

Type: Tandem two-seat primary trainer.

Power Plant: One 400 shp Pratt & Whitney (Canada) PT6A-25 turboprop.

Performance: Max speed, 246 mph (396 km/h) at 17,000 ft (5 180 m); cruising speed, 208 mph (335 km/h) at 1,000 ft (305 m), 233 mph (375 km/h) at 10,000 ft (3 050 m); initial climb, 1,480 ft/min (7,52 m/sec); time to 20,000 ft (6 095 m), 15 min; range, 492 mls (792 km) at 1,000 ft (305 m), 602 mls (970 m) at 10,000 ft (3 050 m), 815 mls (1 312 km) at 20,000 ft (6 095 m).

Weights: Empty, 2,940 lb (1 334 kg); max take-off, 4,300 lb (1 950 kg).

Status: First of two YT-34Cs flown 21 September 1973, with first T-34C for US Navy following in August 1976. Total of 334 ordered for US Navy by beginning of 1984 (with deliveries scheduled for completion April 1984) against total requirement of approximately 450 aircraft.

Notes: Export versions of the basic T-34C are designated Turbine Mentor 34C and (with armament provisions) as the T-34C-1. The latter has been supplied to Argentina (15), Ecuador (23), Gabon (4), Indonesia (16), Morocco (12), Peru (6) and Uruguay (3). The T-34C-1 is suitable for both armament training and light counter-insurgency or close support missions, having four wing ordnance stations of 600 lb (272 kg) capacity inboard and 300 lb (136 kg) outboard, maximum combined load being 1,200 lb (544 kg). Six Turbine Mentor 34Cs have been supplied to Algeria's national pilot training school.

BEECHCRAFT T-34C (TURBINE MENTOR)

Dimensions: Span, 33 ft 4¾ in (10,18 m); length, 28 ft 8½ in (8,75 m); height, 9 ft 10⅞ in (3,02 m); wing area, 179·56 sq ft (16,68 m²).

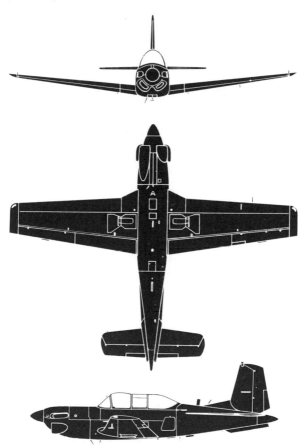

BOEING 737-300

Country of Origin: USA.

Type: Short-haul commercial airliner.

Power Plant: Two 20,000 lb st (9 072 kgp) General Electric CFM56-3 turbofans.

Performance: Max cruise speed, 559 mph (900 km/h) at 25,000 ft (7 620 m); econ cruise, 488 mph (785 km/h) at 35,000 ft (10 670 m); range (with max payload and no reserves), 2,620 mls (4 220 km) at econ cruise, (max fuel and 29,200 lb/13 245 kg payload), 3,410 mls (5 485 km) at 494 mph (795 km/h) at 35,000 ft (10 670 m).

Weights: Operational empty, 69,600 lb (31 570 kg); max take-off, 135,000 lb (61 236 kg).

Accommodation: Flight crew of two and alternative arrangements for 122 to 149 passengers, typical arrangements offering eight first-class seats four abreast and 114 to 120 tourist-class seats six abreast.

Status: First Model 737-300 was scheduled to fly on 2 March 1984, with initial customer deliveries following in November 1984. Some 60 of this version of the Model 737 had been ordered by the beginning of 1984. The 1,000th Model 737 was rolled out on 9 December 1983.

Notes: The Model 737-300 differs from the -200 (see 1983 edition) in having new engines, a 104-in (2,64-m) overall "stretch", strengthened wings and modified wingtips. At the beginning of 1984, consideration was being given to a Model 737-400 with 25,000 lb st (11 340 kgp) CFM56s, a further 100-in (2,54-m) "stretch" and seating for 150 passengers.

BOEING 737-300

Dimensions: Span, 94 ft 9 in (28,90 m); length, 109 ft 7 in (33,40 m); height, 36 ft 6 in (11,12 m); wing area, 980 sq ft (91,04 m²).

BOEING 747-300

Country of Origin: USA.
Type: Long-haul commercial airliner.
Power Plant: Four 54,750 lb st (24 835 kgp) Pratt & Whitney JT9D-7R4G2 turbofans.
Performance: Max cruise speed, 583 mph (939 km/h) at 35,000 ft (10 670 m); econ cruise, 564 mph (907 km/h) at 35,000 ft (10 670 m); long-range cruise, 558 mph (898 km/h); range (max payload at econ cruise), 6,860 mls (11 040 km), (max fuel at long-range cruise), 8,606 mls (13 850 km).
Weights: Operational empty, 389,875 lb (176 847 kg); max take-off, 833,000 lb (377 850 kg).
Accommodation: Normal flight crew of three and up to 69 passengers six-abreast on upper deck, plus basic mixed-class arrangement for 410 passengers, or 415 passengers nine-abreast or 484 10-abreast in economy class seating.
Status: First Model 747-300 flown on 5 October 1982, with first customer delivery (Swissair) March 1983. Total of 616 of all versions of the Model 747 ordered by the beginning of 1984, with 587 delivered and production running at two per month.
Notes: The Model 747-300 differs from the -200 primarily in having a 23-ft (7,0-m) lengthening of the upper deck affording a (typical) 10 per cent increase in total accommodation. Boeing is offering to convert existing Model 747s to -300 standard, the only versions that cannot be modified being the short-fuselage 747SP and those equipped with nose loading doors. The first Model 747-100 was flown on 9 February 1969, and the first Model 747-200 on 11 October 1970. Studies are being pursued of several derivative versions, including introduction of a higher aspect ratio, 250-ft (76,20-m) wing of reduced sweep, and a range of fuselage sizes, with a 25-ft (7,62-m) stretch increasing passenger capacity to a maximum of 650. A new full-length upper deck cabin is also under consideration.

BOEING 747-300

Dimensions: Span, 195 ft 8 in (59,64 m); length, 231 ft 4 in (70,51 m); height, 63 ft 5 in (19,33 m); wing area, 5,685 sq ft (528,15 m²).

BOEING 757-200

Country of Origin: USA.

Type: Short/medium-haul commercial airliner.

Power Plant: Two 37,500 lb st (17 010 kgp) Rolls-Royce RB.211-535C, 38,200 lb st (17 327 kgp) Pratt & Whitney 2037 or 40,100 lb st (18 190 kgp) Rolls-Royce RB.211-535E4 turbofans.

Performance: (RB.211-535C engines) Max cruise speed, 570 mph (917 km/h) at 30,000 ft (9 145 m); econ cruise, 528 mph (850 km/h) at 39,000 ft (11 885 m); range (max payload), 2,210 mls (3 556 km) at econ cruise, (max fuel), 5,343 mls (8 598 km) at long-range cruise.

Weights: Operational empty, 128,450 lb (58 265 kg); max take-off (RB.211-535C engines), 220,000 lb (99 790 kg).

Accommodation: Flight crew of two (with provision for optional third crew member) and typical arrangement of 178 mixed class or 196 tourist class passengers, with max single-class seating for 239 passengers.

Status: First Model 757 flown on 19 February 1982, with first customer deliveries (to Eastern) December 1982 and (British Airways) January 1983. Orders totalling 149 aircraft at beginning of 1984, of which approximately half to be powered by Pratt & Whitney engines with deliveries scheduled from end of 1984. Production rate of two aircraft monthly at beginning of 1984, with total of 28 delivered.

Notes: Two versions of the Model 757 are currently on offer, one with a max take-off weight of 220,000 lb (99 790 kg) and the other for post-1984 delivery with a max take-off weight of 240,000 lb (108 864 kg). The Model 757 is of narrowbody configuration and its wing has been optimised for short-haul routes. At the beginning of 1984, Boeing was engaged in studies of short-range, long-range and combi/convertible freighter versions of the aircraft.

BOEING 757-200

Dimensions: Span, 124 ft 6 in (37,82 m); length, 155 ft 3 in (47,47 m); height, 44 ft 6 in (13,56 m); wing area, 1,951 sq ft (181,25 m²).

BOEING 767-200

Country of Origin: USA.

Type: Medium-haul commercial airliner.

Power Plant: Two 48,000 lb st (21 773 kgp) Pratt & Whitney JT9D-7R4D or General Electric CF6-80A turbofans.

Performance: (JT9D-7R4D engines) Max cruise speed, 556 mph (895 km/h) at 39,000 ft (11 890 m); econ cruise, 528 mph (850 km/h) at 39,000 ft (11 890 m); range (with max payload and no reserves), 2,717 mls (4 373 km) at econ cruise, (max fuel), 6,680 mls (10 750 km).

Weights: (JT9D-7R4D engines) Operational empty, 179,580 lb (81 457 kg); max take-off, 300,000 lb (136 080 kg).

Accommodation: Flight crew of two (with optional three-crew arrangement) and typical mixed-class seating for 18 six-abreast and 193 seven-abreast with two aisles, with max single-class seating for 290 passengers eight-abreast.

Status: First Model 767 (JT9D-7R4D engines) flown on 26 September 1981, (CF6-80A engines) 19 February 1982. First customer delivery (to United) on 18 August 1982, and 80 delivered (to 11 customers) by beginning of 1984, when 189 were on order for 21 customers.

Notes: Three basic versions of the Model 767 were on offer at the beginning of 1984 with 300,000 lb (136 080 kg), 315,000 lb (142 884 kg) and 335,000 lb (151 956 kg) max. take-off weights, the last-mentioned version having 50,000 lb st (22 680 kg) CF6-80A2 engines and a max volume payload range of 4,000 mls (6 437 km). Several variants are under development including a stretched model, the 767-300 with a fuselage lengthened by 21 ft 1 in (6,43 m), and a freighter, weights up to 360,000 lb (163 296 kg) being possible with the present wing and 55,000 lb st (24 948 kgp) engines. The longer-range 767-200ER has been ordered by Ethiopian Airlines, Japan Air Lines, Qantas and the Egyptian government, and the -300 by Japan Air Lines.

BOEING 767-200

Dimensions: Span, 156 ft 4 in (47,65 m); length, 159 ft 2 in (48,50 m); height, 52 ft 0 in (15,85 m); wing area, 3,050 sq ft (283,3 m²).

BOEING E-3 SENTRY

Country of Origin: USA.

Type: Airborne warning and control system aircraft.

Power Plant: Four 21,000 lb st (9 525 kgp) Pratt & Whitney TF33-PW-100A turbofans.

Performance: (At max weight) Average cruise speed, 479 mph (771 km/h) at 28,900-40,100 ft (8 810-12 220 m); average loiter speed, 376 mph (605 km/h) at 29,000 ft (8 840 m); time on station (unrefuelled) at 1,150 mls (1 850 km) from base, 6 hrs, (with one refuelling), 14·4 hrs; ferry range, 5,034 mls (8 100 km) at 475 mph (764 km/h).

Weights: Empty, 170,277 lb (77 238 kg); normal loaded, 214,300 lb (97 206 kg); max take-off, 325,000 lb (147 420 kg).

Accommodation: Operational crew of 17 comprising flight crew of four, systems maintenance team of four, a battle commander and an air defence team of eight.

Status: First of two (EC-137D) development aircraft flown 9 February 1972, two pre-production E-3As following in 1975. First 24 delivered to USAF as E-3As being modified to E-3B standards, and final 10 (including updated third test aircraft) are to be delivered as E-3Cs, the retrofit programme being conducted by the USAF. Eighteen being delivered (in similar configuration to E-3C) to NATO as E-3As with deliveries to be completed June 1985, five CFM56-powered aircraft being delivered to Saudi Arabia from August 1985. Forty E-3s delivered by 1984.

Notes: Aircraft initially delivered to USAF as E-3As are now being fitted with JTIDS (Joint Tactical Information Distribution System), ECM-resistant voice communications, additional HF and UHF radios, austere maritime surveillance capability and more situation display consoles as E-3Bs. The E-3C will feature most E-3B modifications at the production stage, and the E-3As being delivered to NATO are of similar configuration to that of the USAF's E-3C.

BOEING E-3 SENTRY

Dimensions: Span, 145 ft 9 in (44,42 m); length, 152 ft 11 in (46,61 m); height, 42 ft 5 in (12,93 m); wing area, 2,892 sq ft (268,67 m²).

BRITISH AEROSPACE 125-800

Country of Origin: United Kingdom.
Type: Light corporate executive transport.
Power Plant: Two 4,300 lb st (1 950 kgp) Garrett TFE731-5 turbofans.
Performance: Max cruise speed, 533 mph (858 km/h) at 29,000 ft (8 840 m); long-range cruise, 461 mph (741 km/h) at 39,000-43,000 ft (11 900-13 100 m); initial climb, 3,100 ft/min (15,75 m/sec); service ceiling, 43,000 ft (13 100 m); max range (with 1,200-lb/545-kg payload), 3,455 mls (5 560 km) with VFR reserves, 3,005 mls (4 837 km) with IFR reserves.
Weights: Typical operational empty, 15,120 lb (6 858 kg); max take-off, 27,400 lb (12 428 kg).
Accommodation: Pilot and co-pilot on flight deck and standard executive layout for eight passengers in main cabin with optional arrangements for up to 14 seats.
Status: Prototype of Srs 800 flown on 26 May 1983, with certification scheduled for spring 1984. Production scheduled to attain three aircraft monthly by end of 1984.
Notes: The BAe 125-800 is an extensively revised and improved version of the -700 (see 1982 edition) with more powerful engines, new, longer-span outboard wing sections, new ailerons, redesigned flight deck, a larger ventral fuel tank and numerous more minor refinements. Total sales of all versions of the BAe 125 were approaching 570 at the beginning of 1984.

BRITISH AEROSPACE 125-800

Dimensions: Span, 51 ft 4½ in (15,66 m); length, 51 ft 2 in (15,59 m); height, 17 ft 7 in (5,37 m); wing area, 374 sq ft (34,75 m²).

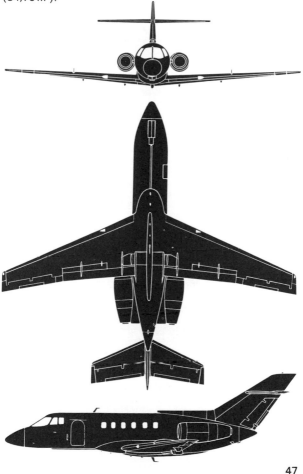

BRITISH AEROSPACE 146-200

Country of Origin: United Kingdom.
Type: Short-haul regional airliner.
Power Plant: Four 6,968 lb st (3 160 kgp) Avco Lycoming ALF 502R-5 turbofans.
Performance: Max cruise speed, 483 mph (778 km/h) at 26,000 ft (7 925 m); econ cruise, 441 mph (710 km/h) at 30,000 ft (9 145 m); long-range cruise, 436 mph (702 km/h) at 30,000 ft (9 145 m); range (max payload), 1,232 mls (1 982 km) at econ cruise, (max fuel), 1,440 mls (2 317 km), or (with optional fuel capacity), 1,727 mls (2 780 km).
Weights: Operational empty, 48,500 lb (22 000 kg); max take-off, 89,500 lb (40 597 kg).
Accommodation: Flight crew of two and maximum seating (single-class) for 106 passengers six-abreast.
Status: First BAe 146-100 flown 3 September 1981, and first BAe 146-200 flown on 1 August 1982, with first customer deliveries of -100 (Dan Air) early 1983, and -200 (Air Wisconsin) March 1983. Eight -100s and 30 -200s ordered by beginning of 1984, plus 45 on option, and production rate of two aircraft monthly at beginning of 1984.
Notes: The BAe 146 is currently being manufactured in -100 form with an 85 ft 10 in (26,16 m) fuselage for up to 82 passengers (illustrated above) and -200 form (described). The BAe 146 is optimised for operation over stage lengths of the order of 150 miles (240 km) with unrefuelled multi-stop capability. Apart from fuselage length and capacity, the two versions of the BAe 146 are similar in all respects, but the uprated R-5 version of the ALF 502 turbofan is available for the longer -200 model which is featured by most initial orders. Various military versions of the BAe 146 have been considered, some featuring rear freight loading ramp, and two -100 models have been delivered to the RAF for evaluation.

BRITISH AEROSPACE 146-200

Dimensions: Span, 85 ft 5 in (26,34 m); length, 93 ft 8½ in (28,56 m); height, 28 ft 3 in (8,61 m); wing area, 832 sq ft (77,30 m²).

BRITISH AEROSPACE HAWK

Country of Origin: United Kingdom.

Type: Tandem two-seat basic/advanced trainer and light tactical aircraft.

Power Plant: One 5,200 lb st (2 360 kgp) Rolls-Royce Turboméca Adour 151, or (Srs 60) 5,700 lb st (2 585 kgp) Adour 861 turbofan.

Performance: (T Mk 1) Max speed (clean aircraft with one crew member) 622 mph (1 000 km/h) or Mach 0·815 at sea level, 580 mph (933 km/h) or Mach 0·88 at 36,000 ft (10 970 m); max climb, 11,833 ft/min (60,1 m/sec); tactical radius (with four 550-lb/250 kg bombs and two 130 Imp gal/590 l drop tanks), 680 mls (1 095 km) HI-LO-HI, 317 mls (510 km) LO-LO-LO.

Weights: Empty, 8,000 lb (3 629 kg); loaded (clean), 11,100 lb (5 040 kg); max take-off (ground attack), 18,390 lb (8 342 kg).

Armament: (Srs 100) Five external ordnance stations for max. of 6,800 lb (3 100 kg) when flown as single-seater. Seventy-two Hawk T Mk 1s were being modified at beginning of 1984 to carry two AIM-9 Sidewinder AAMs to provide secondary air defence capability.

Status: Pre-series Hawk flown 21 August 1974, with first of 175 for RAF flown 19 May 1975. Export versions include Mk 51 (Finland, 50), Mk 52 (Kenya, 12), Mk 53 (Indonesia, 20), Mk 60 (Zimbabwe, 8), Mk 61 (Dubai, 8), Mk 63 (Abu Dhabi, 16) and Mk 64 (Kuwait, 12). The T-45A is a carrier-capable development of the Hawk for the US Navy, scheduled to fly in 1988. The T-45 is being developed jointly with McDonnell Douglas, the US Navy having a requirement for 300 T-45As. Currently on offer is the Series 100, which, similarly powered to the Series 60, has an inertial navigator, headup display, laser rangefinder and a weapon aiming computer. The Hawk is now able to carry the BAe Sea Eagle anti-ship missile.

BRITISH AEROSPACE HAWK

Dimensions: Span, 30 ft 9¾ in (9,39 m); length, 38 ft 10⅔ in (11,85 m); height, 13 ft 1 in (4,00 m); wing area, 179·64 sq ft (16,69 m²).

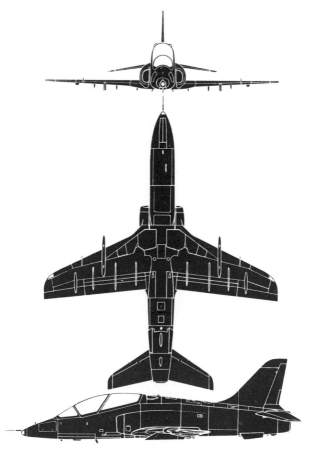

BRITISH AEROSPACE JETSTREAM 31

Country of Origin: United Kingdom.
Type: Light corporate transport and regional airliner.
Power Plant: Two 900 shp Garrett TPE 331-10 turboprops.
Performance: Max cruise speed, 299 mph (482 km/h) at 20,000 ft (6 100 m); long-range cruise, 265 mph (426 km/h) at 25,000 ft (7 620 m); initial climb, 2,200 ft min (11,2 m/sec); max range (with 19 passengers and IFR reserves), 737 mls (1 186 km), (with 12 passengers), 1,094 mls (1 760 km), (with nine passengers), 1,324 mls (2 130 km).
Weights: Empty equipped (including flight crew), 8,840 lb (4 010 kg); max take-off, 14,550 lb (6 600 kg).
Accommodation: Two seats side by side on flight deck with basic corporate executive seating for eight passengers, with optional 12-seat executive shuttle arrangement, or up to 19 passengers three-abreast with offset aisle in high-density regional airline arrangement.
Status: First Jetstream 31 flown on 18 March 1982, following flight development aircraft (converted from a Series 1 airframe) flown on 28 March 1980. First customer delivery (Contactair of Stuttgart) made 15 December 1982. Jetstream 31 sales commitments totalled 24 aircraft by the beginning of 1984, in which year production is planned to attain a minimum of 25 aircraft. Some 18 aircraft were completed during the course of 1983.
Notes: The Jetstream 31 is a derivative of the Handley Page H.P.137 Jetstream, the original prototype of which was flown on 18 August 1967. An inshore maritime patrol version, the Jetstream 31EZ (Economic Zone) was under development at the beginning of 1984, this having 360-deg scan search radar, a searchlight and a crew of five.

52

BRITISH AEROSPACE JETSTREAM 31

Dimensions: Span, 52 ft 0 in (15,85 m); length, 47 ft 2 in (14,37 m); height, 17 ft 6 in (5,37 m); wing area, 270 sq ft (25,08 m²).

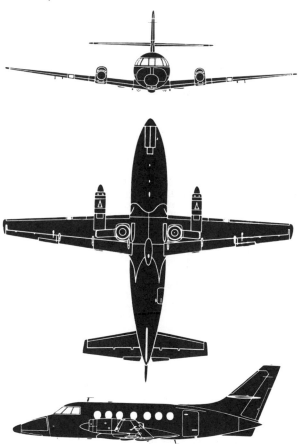

BRITISH AEROSPACE NIMROD MR MK 2

Country of Origin: United Kingdom.

Type: Long-range maritime patrol aircraft.

Power Plant: Four 12,160 lb st (5515 kgp) Rolls-Royce RB.168-20 Spey Mk 250 turbofans.

Performance: Max speed, 575 mph (926 km/h); max transit speed, 547 mph (880 km/h); econ transit speed, 490 mph (787 km/h); typical ferry range, 5,180-5,755 mls (8340-9265 km); typical endurance, 12 hrs; maximum (with one flight refuelling and two additional crew members), 19 hrs.

Weights: Max take-off, 184,000 lb (83 460 kg); max overload, 192,000 lb (87 090 kg).

Armament: Ventral weapons bay accommodating full range of ASW weapons (e.g, Stingray homing torpedoes, mines, depth charges). Provision for two underwing pylons on each side for Aérospatiale AS 12 Harpoon or Sea Eagle anti-shipping missiles.

Accommodation: Normal operating crew of 12 with two pilots and flight engineer on flight deck, and nine sensor operators and navigators in tactical compartment.

Status: Thirty-two Nimrod MR Mk 1s are being progressively brought up to MR Mk 2 standard in a programme scheduled to continue until mid-1984, the first MR Mk 2 production conversion having flown on 13 February 1979. The first of 46 Nimrod MR Mk 1s was flown on 28 June 1968, 11 of these being allocated to the AEW Mk 3 programme (see pages 56–57). In addition, three Nimrods have been supplied to the RAF as R Mk 1s for electronic reconnaissance duties.

Notes: The Nimrod MR Mk 2 possesses 60 times more computer power than the MR Mk 1 that it supplants in RAF service, and is equipped with the advanced Searchwater pulse compression maritime radar, an AQS-901 acoustic system compatible with the Barra sonobuoy, and EWSM (Electronic Warfare Support Measures) in wingtip pods. During 1982, 16 Nimrod MR Mk 2s were fitted with air refuelling provisions (as illustrated) as a result of Falklands experience.

BRITISH AEROSPACE NIMROD MR MK 2

Dimensions: Span, 114 ft 10 in (35,00 m); length, 126 ft 9 in (38,63 m); height, 29 ft 8½ in (9,01 m); wing area, 2,121 sq ft (197,05 m²).

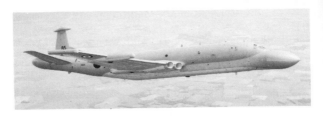

BRITISH AEROSPACE NIMROD AEW MK 3

Country of Origin: United Kingdom.
Type: Airborne warning and control system aircraft.
Power Plant: Four 12,160 lb st (5 515 kgp) Rolls-Royce RB.168-20 Spey Mk 250 turbofans.
Performance: No details have been released for publication, but maximum and transit speeds are likely to be generally similar to those of the MR Mk 2 (see pages 54–55), and maximum endurance is in excess of 10 hours. The mission requirement calls for 6–7 hours on station at 29,000-35,000 ft (8 840-10 670 m) at approx 350 mph (563 km/h) at 750-1,000 miles (1 120-1 600 km) from base.
Weights: Max take-off (approx), 190,000 lb (85 185 kg).
Accommodation: Flight crew of four and tactical team of six, latter comprising tactical air control officer, communications control officer, EWSM (Electronic Warfare Support Measures) operator and three air direction officers.
Status: Total of 11 Nimrod MR Mk 1 airframes being rebuilt to AEW Mk 3 standard of which fully representative prototype flew on 16 July 1980. The Nimrod AEW Mk 3 is scheduled to enter service with the RAF during 1984, five rebuilt airframes having been flown by the beginning of the year with the first having been scheduled for handover in February 1984.
Notes: The Nimrod AEW Mk 3 is equipped with Marconi mission system avionics with identical radar aerials mounted in nose and tail, these being synchronised and each sequentially sweeping through 180 deg in azimuth in order to provide uninterrupted coverage throughout the 360 deg of combined sweep. EWSM pods are located at the wingtips and weather radar in the starboard wing pinion tank. The Nimrod AEW Mk 3 is intended to provide complementary capability with the Boeing E-3A Sentries operated by the NATO combined force (excluding the UK).

BRITISH AEROSPACE NIMROD AEW MK 3

Dimensions: Span, 115 ft 1 in (35,08 m); length, 137 ft 8½ in (41,97 m); height, 35 ft 0 in (10,67 m); wing area, 2,121 sq ft (197,05 m²).

BRITISH AEROSPACE SEA HARRIER

Country of Origin: United Kingdom.
Type: Single-seat V/STOL shipboard multi-role fighter.
Power Plant: One 21,500 lb st (9 760 kgp) Rolls-Royce
Pegasus 104 vectored-thrust turbofan.
Performance: Max speed (clean aircraft), 720 mph
(1 160 km/h) or Mach 0·95 at 1,000 ft (305 m), 607 mph
(977 km/h) or Mach 0·92 at 36,000 ft (10 970 m), (with two
AIM-9L AAMs and two Martel ASMs), 598 mph (962 km/h)
or Mach 0·83 at sea level; combat radius (recce mission with
two 100 Imp gal/455 l drop tanks), 518 mls (520 km); endurance (with two drop tanks for combat air patrol), 1·5 hrs at
115 mls/185 km from ship with three min combat.
Weights: Empty (approx), 13,000 lb (5 897 kg); normal
loaded (STO), 21,700 lb (9 840 kg); max take-off 25,600 lb
(11 612 kg).
Armament: Provision for two 30-mm cannon plus two AIM-
9L Sidewinder AAMs and up to 5,000 lb (2 268 kg) ordnance
on five external stations.
Status: First Sea Harrier (built on production tooling) flown
on 21 August 1978, with deliveries against initial 34 ordered
for Royal Navy completed during 1982 when follow-on batch
of 14 aircraft ordered. Six (FRS Mk 51) ordered for Indian Navy
with completion of deliveries early 1984.
Notes: The Royal Navy's Sea Harrier FRS Mk 1 is a derivative
of the RAF's Harrier GR Mk 3 (see 1982 edition) to operate
from *Invincible*-class through-deck cruisers. Changes for the
naval role include a new forward fuselage with raised cockpit,
nose installation of Blue Fox intercept radar, new operational
equipment and various changes to airframe and engine to suit
maritime environment. During 1983, proposals were made for
a mid-life update of the Sea Harrier involving installation of a
new pulse doppler radar. redesigned wing tips to provide two
additional missile stations and provision for new missiles.

BRITISH AEROSPACE SEA HARRIER

Dimensions: Span, 25 ft 3 in (7,70 m); length, 47 ft 7 in (14,50 m); height, 12 ft 2 in (3,70 m); wing area, 201·1 sq ft (18,68 m²).

BRITISH AEROSPACE VC10 K MK 2

Country of Origin: United Kingdom.

Type: Flight refuelling tanker.

Power Plant: Four 21,800 lb st (9 888 kgp) Rolls-Royce Conway Mk 550B turbofans.

Performance: Max cruising speed, 568 mph (914 km/h); long-range cruise, 425 mph (684 km/h) at 30,000 ft (9 150 m); initial climb, 3,050 ft/min (15,5 m/sec); approx range, 3,900 mls (6 275 km).

Weights: Max take-off (approx), 323,000 lb (146 510 kg).

Accommodation: Primary flight crew of four comprising pilot, co-pilot, navigator and flight engineer. Compartment for 18 personnel in aft-facing seating.

Status: First VC10 K Mk 2 (conversion of of VC10 Model 1101) flown 22 June 1982, and four similar conversions of the standard commercial VC10, plus four conversions of Super VC10 Model 1154s as K Mk 3s, for the RAF. Three K Mk 2s delivered by beginning of 1984, and K Mk 3 deliveries scheduled to commence August 1984, with completion in January 1985. Further VC10s will be converted as funding permits.

Notes: During 1958, the RAF initiated a programme to convert commercial VC10s as three-point tankers, this including both standard VC10s and the lengthened (171 ft 8 in/52,32 m) Super VC10s as K Mk 2s and K Mk 3s respectively, engine commonality being achieved and a common installation of fuselage fuel cells being adopted. After modification, the two versions of the tanker are assigned new Type numbers by British Aerospace, the K Mk 2s being Type 1112s and the K Mk 3s being Type 1164s. Fuel for refuelling operations is housed by five double-skinned cylindrical tanks. Flight Refuelling Mk 32 hose-and-drogue pods are mounted beneath the wings and a Flight Refuelling Mk 17B HDU is installed in the rear fuselage to provide three-point refuelling.

BRITISH AEROSPACE VC10 K MK 2

Dimensions: Span, 146 ft 2 in (44,55 m); length (excluding refuelling probe), 158 ft 8 in (48,36 m); height, 39 ft 6 in (12,04 m); wing area, 2,932 sq ft (272,4 m²).

CANADAIR CHALLENGER 601

Country of Origin: Canada.

Type: Light corporate transport.

Power Plant: Two 9,140 lb st (4 146 kgp) with 5-min limit or 8,650 lb st (3 924 kgp) General Electric CF34-1A turbofans.

Performance: Max cruise speed, 528 mph (850 km/h) or Mach 0·8; normal cruise, 507 mph (819 km/h) or Mach 0·77; range cruise, 488 mph (786 km/h) or Mach 0·74; operational ceiling, 41,000 ft (12 500 m); max range (with passengers and IFR reserves), 3,982 mls (6 408 km).

Weights: Empty, 19,960 lb (9 054 kg); operational empty (typical), 24,525 lb (11 124 kg); max take-off, 42,100 lb (19 097 kg).

Accommodation: Flight crew of two with typical main cabin executive configurations for 8–11 passengers.

Status: Prototype Challenger 601 flown on 10 April 1982, with FAA certification following on 25 February 1983, and production proceeding at 1·5 monthly at beginning of 1984.

Notes: The Challenger 601 is the intercontinental-range derivative of the transcontinental Challenger 600, the latter differing in having 7,500 lb st (3 402 kgp) Avco Lycoming ALF 502L turbofans and lacking the winglets featured by the later model (although these are now being offered as a retrofit). A total of 82 Challenger 600s had been completed mid-1983 when further production of this version was temporarily suspended. Max take-off weight of the Challenger 601 is being increased to 43,100 lb (19 550 kg) which will increase full fuel payload from 1,000 lb (454 kg) to 1,700 lb (771 kg).

CANADAIR CHALLENGER 601

Dimensions: Span, 64 ft 4 in (19,61 m); length, 68 ft 5 in (20,85 m); height, 20 ft 8 in (6,30 m) wing area (basic), 450 sq ft (41,82 m²).

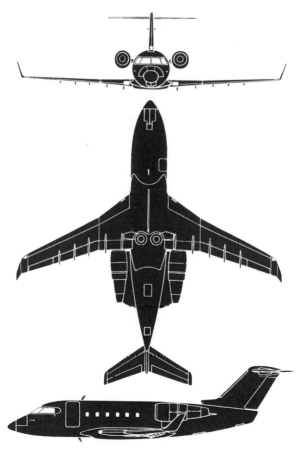

CASA C-101 AVIOJET

Country of Origin: Spain.
Type: Tandem two-seat basic/advanced trainer and light tactical support aircraft.
Power Plant: One (C-101EB) 3,500 lb st (1 588 kgp) Garrett AiResearch TFE 731-2-2J or (C-101BB) 3,700 lb st (1 678 kgp) TFE 731-3-1J turbofan.
Performance: (C-101BB) Max speed (clean aircraft), 432 mph (695 km/h) at sea level, 495 mph (797 km/h) at 25,000 ft (7 620 m); initial climb, 3,800 ft/min (19,3 m/sec); time to 25,000 ft (7 620 m), 8·5 min; tactical radius (with four 550-lb/250-kg bombs and 30-mm cannon on internal fuel with 10 min reserves), 207 mls (333 km) LO-LO-LO interdiction.
Weights: (C-101BB) Empty equipped, 7,496 lb (3 400 kg); max take-off, 12,346 lb (5 600 kg).
Armament: (C-101BB) One 30-mm cannon or two 12,7-mm machine guns plus max. of 3,307 lb (1 500 kg) of ordnance distributed between six wing stations.
Status: First of four prototypes flown 29 June 1977, with deliveries to Spanish Air Force against orders for 88 C-101EB trainers commencing March 1980, and some 80 delivered by beginning of 1984. First C-101BB delivered to Chile in August 1981 as T-36. Chilean requirement for 60 aircraft of which 16 ordered and first four delivered complete with remaining aircraft being assembled in Chile by INDAER with progressive Chilean manufacturing participation. First of four C-101CC dedicated attack model for Chile flown in October 1983, and four C-101BB Aviojets ordered by Honduras for 1984 delivery.
Notes: The C-101EB pilot trainer and dual-role C-101BB are similar apart from engine power and armament provisions. Versions of the Aviojet with more advanced equipment (eg, head-up display and low-level Doppler navigation system) were under development at beginning of 1984.

CASA C-101 AVIOJET

Dimensions: Span, 34 ft 9⅜ in (10,60 m); length, 40 ft 2¼ in (12,25 m); height, 13 ft 11 in (4,25 m); wing area, 215·3 sq ft (20,00 m²).

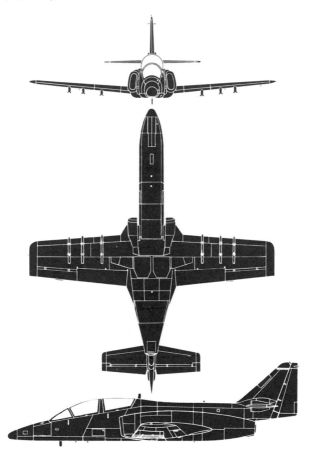

CASA-NURTANIO CN-235

Countries of Origin: Spain and Indonesia.
Type: Regional airliner, freighter and mixed passenger/freight transport.
Power Plant: Two 1,772 eshp General Electric GT-7-7 turboprops.
Performance: Max cruising speed (at 27,225 lb/12 349 kg), 282 mph (455 km/h) at 15,000 ft (4 570 m); initial climb, 1,780 ft/min (9,04 m/sec); range (max payload with IFR reserves), 497 mls (800 km) at 15,000 ft (4 570 m); max range (with 1,819 lb/825 kg payload), 2,417 mls (3 890 km).
Weights: Empty equipped, 17,526 lb (7 950 kg); operational empty, 18,133 lb (8 225 kg); max take-off, 28,658 lb (13 000 kg).
Accommodation: Flight crew of two and standard seating arrangements for 35 or 39 passengers four-abreast with central aisle. As a freighter LD-3 containers and 88-in (2,23-m) pallets may be accommodated to max of 9,920 lb (4 500 kg).
Status: First prototype flown on 11 November and second on 31 December 1983, with first delivery (to Aviaco) scheduled for December 1984. Assembly lines in both Spain and Indonesia expected to deliver a combined total of 26 during 1985, 53 in 1986, and 66 in 1987. Both lines scheduled to produce up to three monthly. Total of 106 (plus 23 options) on order by beginning of 1984.
Notes: The CN-235 is being built jointly by CASA of Spain and Nurtanio of Indonesia on a 50-50 basis without component manufacturing duplication. Thirty-two have been ordered by the Indonesian Air Force and 18 by the Indonesian naval air component primarily for the logistic support, personnel transportation and aeromedical tasks.

CASA-NURTANIO CN-235

Dimensions: Span, 84 ft 7⅜ in (25,81 m); length, 70 ft 0⅝ in (21,35 m); height, 26 ft 9¾ in (8,18 m); wing area, 636·17 sq ft (59,10 m²).

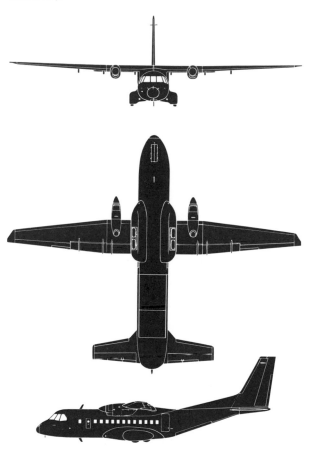

CESSNA 208 CARAVAN I

Country of Origin: USA.
Type: Light utility transport.
Power Plant: One 600 shp Pratt & Whitney (Canada) PT6A-114 turboprop.
Performance: Max cruise speed, 214 mph (345 km/h); initial climb, 1,446 ft/min (7,4 m/sec); service ceiling, 30,000 ft (9 150 m); range (at max cruise with allowances and 45-min reserve), 1,147 mls (1 846 km).
Weights: Standard empty, 3,415 lb (1 549 kg); max take-off, 7,000 lb (3 175 kg).
Accomodation: Pilot and up to 13 passengers in a combination of two- and three-abreast seating with aisle between seats.
Status: Prototype Caravan I flown on 9 December 1982, with first production-standard aircraft to fly in July 1984, with certification following in October, and customer deliveries commencing thereafter. Planned production rate of 100 annually.
Notes: To be certificated with specially-design Wipline amphibious floats and suitable for operation with skis, the Caravan I is claimed to be the first all-new single-turboprop aircraft designed for the utility role. Rapidly convertible from all-passenger to passenger-and-freight or all-freight configurations, the Caravan I has four doors in the fuselage, including a large cargo door, and has an airstair door for passengers in the starboard rear of the cabin. The cabin can accommodate such loads as two D-size cargo containers or up to 10 fuel drums of 55 US gal (208 l) capacity, and optional installations enable the Caravan I to be used for aerial firefighting, agricultural spraying, aerial photography, supply dropping and aeromedical applications.

CESSNA 208 CARAVAN I

Dimensions: Span, 51 ft 8 in (15,75 m); length, 37 ft 7 in (11,45 m); height, 14 ft 2 in (4,29 m); wing area, 279·52 sq ft (25,97 m²).

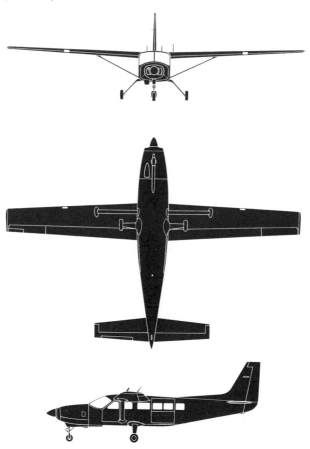

CESSNA 550 CITATION SII

Country of Origin: USA.

Type: Light corporate transport.

Power Plant: Two 2,500 lb st (1 134 kgp) Pratt & Whitney (Canada) JT15D-4B turbofans.

Performance: Cruising speed, 463 mph (746 km/h) at 35,000 ft (10,670 m); time to 35,000 ft (10 670 m), 21 min; max altitude, 43,000 ft (13 105 m); range (with eight occupants and 45 min reserves), 2,060 mls (3 315 km).

Weights: Standard empty, 7,716 lb (3 500 kg); max takeoff, 14,300 lb (6 487 kg).

Accommodation: Pilot and co-pilot/passenger on flight deck and six-eight passengers in individual seats in main cabin.

Status: First announced in October 1983, the Citation SII is an improved development of the Citation II and was succeeding the earlier model on the assembly line at the beginning of 1984, with customer deliveries scheduled to commence spring 1984.

Notes: The Citation SII introduces a new aerofoil section reducing high-speed drag, an extended inboard wing leading edge increasing lift and fuel volume, higher thrust engines, modified flaps, which, like the ailerons, are of graphite composite, and numerous other refinements. The original Citation II (illustrated above) flew on 31 January 1977, customer deliveries commencing in the spring of 1978, some 400 having since been delivered. Fifteen Citation IIs are being supplied to the US Navy as T-47As for tactical navigator and radar intercept officer training.

CESSNA 550 CITATION SII

Dimensions: Span, 52 ft 2¼ in (15,90 m); length, 47 ft 2¼ in (14,40 m); height, 15 ft 0 in (4,57 m); wing area, 342·6 sq ft (31,70 m²).

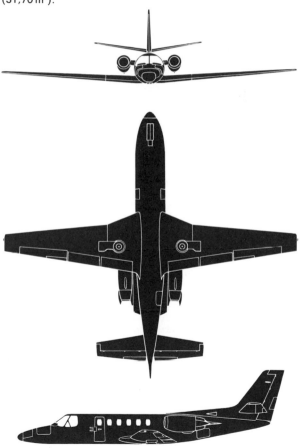

CESSNA 650 CITATION III

Country of Origin: USA.
Type: Light corporate transport.
Power Plant: Two 3,650 lb st (1 656 kgp) Garrett TFE731-3B-100S turbofans.
Performance: Max cruise speed (at 16,000 lb/7 258 kg), 544 mph (875 km/h) at 35,000 ft (10 670 m), 528 mph (850 km/h) at 41,000 ft (12 500 m); time to 35,000 ft (10 670 m) at 20,000 lb (9 072 kg), 14 min; range (with six passengers and 45 min reserve), 3,040 mls (4 894 km) at 482 mph (776 km/h) at 45,000 ft (13 715 m); ferry range, 3,200 mls (5 150 km).
Weights: Operational empty (average), 12,200 lb (5 534 kg); max take-off, 21,000 lb (9 526 kg).
Accommodation: Normal flight crew of two on flight deck and standard main cabin arrangement for six passengers in individual seats.
Status: Two prototypes flown on 30 May 1979 and 2 May 1980 respectively, with certification following on 30 April 1982, and customer deliveries commencing early 1983. Nineteen delivered to 1 October 1983, with production rising to five monthly and 60 scheduled for delivery during following 12 months. Production rate of seven monthly anticipated in 1985.
Notes: The Citation III owes nothing to preceding Citations despite its name, being of all new aerodynamic design and featuring a supercritical wing. The first production model established two time-to-altitude records in 1983 for aircraft in its class and a record by flying from Gander to Le Bourget in 5 hr 13 min.

CESSNA 650 CITATION III

Dimensions: Span, 53 ft 3½ in (16,30 m); length, 55 ft 6 in (16,90 m); height, 17 ft 3½ in (5,30 m); wing area, 312 sq ft (29,00 m²).

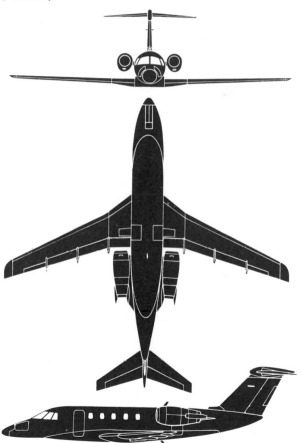

DASSAULT-BREGUET ATLANTIC G2 (ATL2)

Country of Origin: France.

Type: Long-range maritime patrol aircraft.

Power Plant: Two 5,665 shp Rolls-Royce/SNECMA Tyne RTy 20 Mk 21 turboprops.

Performance: Max speed, 368 mph (593 km/h) at sea level; normal cruise, 345 mph (556 km/h) at 25,000 ft (7 620 m); typical patrol speed, 196 mph (315 km/h); initial climb, 2,000 ft/min (10,1 m/sec); service ceiling, 30,000 ft (9 100 m); typical mission, 8 hrs patrol at 690 mls (1 110 km) from base at 2,000-3,000 ft (610-915 m); max range, 5,590 mls (9 000 km).

Weights: Empty equipped, 56,217 lb (25 500 kg); normal loaded weight, 97,885 lb (44 400 kg); max take-off, 101,850 lb (46 200 kg).

Accommodation: Normal flight crew of 12, comprising two pilots, flight engineer, forward observer, radio navigator, ESM/ECM/MAD operator, radar operator, tactical co-ordinator, two acoustic operators and two aft observers.

Armament: Up to eight Mk 46 homing torpedoes, nine 550-lb (250-kg) bombs or 12 depth charges, plus two AM 39 Exocet ASMs in forward weapons bay. Four wing stations with combined capacity of 7,715 lb (3 500 kg).

Status: First of two prototypes (converted from ATL1s) flown 8 May 1981, with second following on 26 March 1982, decision to manufacture 32 for France's *Aéronavale* announced June 1982, with production launch in 1984, and first deliveries scheduled for 1988.

Notes: The Atlantic G2 (*Génération* 2), also referred to as the ATL2, is a modernised version of the Atlantic G1 (now referred to as the ATL1), production of which terminated in 1973 after completion of 87 series aircraft. By comparison with the ATL1, the ATL2 has upgraded systems and refined structure.

DASSAULT-BREGUET ATLANTIC G2 (ATL2)

Dimensions: Span, 122 ft 7 in (37,36 m); length, 107 ft 0$\frac{1}{4}$ in (36,62 m); height, 37 ft 1$\frac{1}{4}$ in (11,31 m); wing area, 1,295·3 sq ft (120,34 m²).

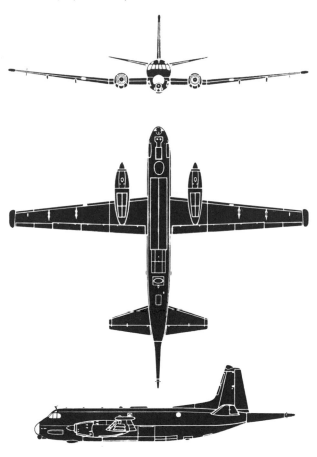

DASSAULT-BREGUET
MYSTERE-FALCON 900

Country of Origin: France.

Type: Light corporate transport.

Power Plant: Three 4,500 lb st (2 040 kgp) Garrett TFE 731-5A turbofans.

Performance: (Estimated) Max cruise, 554 mph (892 km/h) or Mach 0·84 at 39,000 ft (11 890 m); range cruise, 495 mph (797 km/h) or Mach 0·75 at 37,000 ft (11 275 m); range (with eight passengers at long-range cruise with IFR reserves), 4,375 mls (7 040 km), (with 19 passengers), 3,915 mls (6 300 km), (with max payload), 2,765 mls (4 450 km); max cruise altitude, 51,000 ft (15 550 m).

Weights: Operational empty, 23,400 lb (10 615 kg); max take-off, 45,500 lb (20 640 kg).

Accommodation: Flight crew of two on flight deck and various arrangements in main cabin for 8–15 passengers. Optional arrangements for 19 passengers and provision included in basic design for additional emergency exits which will permit up to 34 passengers to be carried in a high-density configuration for airline operation.

Status: Prototype scheduled to commence flight test October 1984, with certification following in 1985 and initial customer deliveries mid-1986.

Notes: The Mystère-Falcon 900 is a derivative of the Mystère-Falcon 50 (see 1982 edition) with which it shares some component commonality, but it features a longer, larger-diameter fuselage, longer span wing, higher-powered engines and various aerodynamic refinements. The Mystère-Falcon 900 possesses a larger cross-section cabin than the forthcoming Gulfstream IV and a longer cabin than the Canadair Challenger, its principal competitors, and fuel burn will allegedly be 25 per cent less than that of the Gulfstream IV over a comparable range.

DASSAULT-BREGUET MYSTERE-FALCON 900

Dimensions: Span, 63 ft 5 in (19,33 m); length, 66 ft 5¼ in (20,25 m); height, 24 ft 9¼ in (7,55 m); wing area, 527·77 sq ft (49,03 m²).

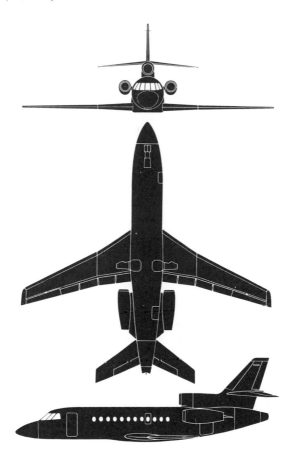

DASSAULT-BREGUET MIRAGE F1

Country of Origin: France.
Type: Single-seat multi-role fighter.
Power Plant: One 11,023 lb st (5 000 kgp) dry and 15,873 lb st (7 200 kgp) reheat SNECMA Atar 9K50 turbojet.
Performance: (F1C) Max speed (clean aircraft), 914 mph (1 470 km/h) or Mach 1·2 at sea level, 1,450 mph (2 555 km/h) or Mach 2·2 at 39,370 ft (12 000 m); initial climb, 41,930 ft/min (213 m/sec); service ceiling, 65,600 ft (20 000 m); tactical radius (with two drop tanks and 4,410 lb/2 000 kg bombs), 670 mls (1 078 km).
Weights: Empty, 16,314 lb (7 400 kg); normal loaded, 24,030 lb (10 900 kg); max take-off, 32,850 lb (14 900 kg).
Armament: Two 30-mm DEFA 553 cannon and (intercept) one-three Matra 550 Magic plus two AIM-9 AAMs, or (close support) up to 8,818 lb (4 000 kg) of external ordnance.
Status: First of four prototypes flown 23 December 1966, and first production aircraft flown 15 February 1973, with 600 delivered by beginning of 1984 and production continuing at five monthly.
Notes: Current production models for the *Armée de l'Air* consist of the F1C-200 with fixed flight refuelling probe, the tactical recce F1CR (illustrated above) and the two-seat F1B conversion trainer. Whereas the F1C is an optimised air-air version, the export F1A and F1E are optimised for the air-ground role. The two-seat model retains the Cyrano IV radar, weapon system and missile capability of the F1C, but has no internal guns and fuel capacity is reduced. Foreign orders for the F1 are Ecuador (18), Iraq (89), Jordan (36), Qatar (14), Kuwait (32), Libya (38), Morocco (50), Greece (40), South Africa (48) and Spain (73). The *Armée de l'Air* is receiving 231 Mirage F1s, comprising 170 F1Cs, 41 F1CRs and 20 F1Bs with deliveries to be completed during 1984.

DASSAULT-BREGUET MIRAGE F1

Dimensions: Span, 27 ft 6¾ in (8,40 m); length, 49 ft 2½ in (15,00 m); height, 14 ft 9 in (4,50 m); wing area, 269·1 sq ft (25,00 m²).

DASSAULT-BREGUET MIRAGE 2000

Country of Origin: France.

Type: Single-seat multi-role fighter.

Power Plant: One 12,345 lb st (5 600 kgp) dry and 19,840 lb st (9 000 kgp) reheat SNECMA M53-5, or (from 1985) 14,460 lb st (6 560 kgp) dry and 21,385 lb st (9 700 kgp) reheat M53-P2 turbofan.

Performance: Max speed (clean aircraft), 915 mph (1 472 km/h) or Mach 1·2 at sea level, 1,550 mph (2 495 km/h) or Mach 2·35 (short endurance dash) above 36,090 ft (11 000 m); max. climb, 49,000 ft/min (249 m/sec); service ceiling, 59,055 ft (18 000 m); combat radius (intercept mission with two drop tanks and four AAMs), 435 mls (700 km).

Weights: Loaded (clean), 20,944 lb (9 500 kg); max take-off, 33,070 lb (15 000 kg).

Armament: Two 30-mm DEFA 554 cannon and (air superiority) two Matra 550 Magic and two Matra Super 530D AAMs, or (close support) up to 13,227 lb (6 000 kg) of ordnance distributed between nine stations.

Status: First of five prototypes (four single-seat and one two-seat) flown 10 March 1978, with first production Mirage 2000C flown 20 November 1982. By the beginning of 1984, 78 had been funded against anticipated *Armée de l'Air* requirement for 243 to 1988 in three main versions. Orders placed during 1982 by Egypt (20), Peru (26), India (40), and in 1983 by Abu Dhabi (18). The first two-seat Mirage 2000N (*Nucléaire*) flew on 3 February 1983, funding for 15 of this version (for 1988 delivery) included in 1983 budget. A production rate of three monthly was attained by the beginning of 1984.

Notes: The Mirage 2000 is to be adopted by the *Armée de l'Air* in single-seat air superiority and attack, and two-seat conversion training and low-level penetration versions, deliveries commenced late 1983 with service entry following at Dijon during December of that year.

DASSAULT-BREGUET MIRAGE 2000

Dimensions: Span, 29 ft 6 in (9,00 m); length, 47 ft $6\frac{7}{8}$ in (14,50 m); wing area, 441·3 sq ft (41,00 m²).

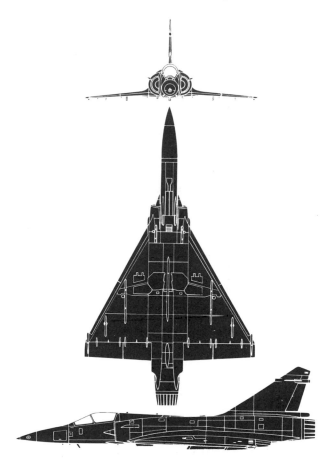

DASSAULT-BREGUET/DORNIER ALPHA JET

Countries of Origin: France and Federal Germany.

Type: Tandem two-seat basic/advanced trainer and light tactical support aircraft.

Power Plant: Two 2,975 lb st (1 350 kgp) SNECMA-Turboméca Larzac 04-C5 or (NGEA) 3,360 lb st (1 525 kgp) 04-C20 turbofans.

Performance: (Larzac 04-C5) Max speed (clean aircraft), 622 mph (1 000 km/h) or Mach 0·82 at sea level, 567 mph (912 km/h) or Mach 0·84 at 32,810 ft (10 000 m); max. climb, 11,220 ft/min (57 m/sec); tactical radius (training mission), 267 mls (430 km) at low altitude, 683 mls (1 100 km) at high altitude; ferry range (max. external fuel), 1,785 mls (2 872 km).

Weights: Empty, 7,716 lb (3 500 kg); loaded (clean), 11,023 lb (5 000 kg); max take-off, 15,983 lb (7 250 kg).

Armament: (Close air support) External centreline gun pod with (Alpha Jet E) 30-mm DEFA 533 or (Alpha Jet A) 27-mm Mauser cannon, plus up to 4,850 lb (2 200 kg) of ordnance on four wing stations.

Status: First prototype flown 26 October 1973, with 440 delivered by beginning of 1984 against 499 ordered as follows: France (175), Germany (175), Belgium (33), Cameroun (6), Egypt (45), Ivory Coast (6), Morocco (24), Nigeria (24), Qatar (6) and Togo (5). Final assembly lines in Toulouse, Munich and (for Egyptian Air Force) Helwan.

Notes: Manufactured under joint Franco-German programme with French version optimised for training and German version for close air support. Alpha Jet NGEA (*Nouvelle Génération Ecole-Appui*) with enhanced weapon system (illustrated) entered flight test in April 1982. This version has been ordered by Egypt (15) and Cameroun (6). It features uprated Larzac engines and an integrated nav/attack system.

DASSAULT-BREGUET/DORNIER ALPHA JET

Dimensions: Span, 29 ft 11 in (9,11 m); length, 40 ft 3 in (12,29 m); height, 13 ft 9 in (4,19 m); wing area, 188 sq ft (17,50 m²).

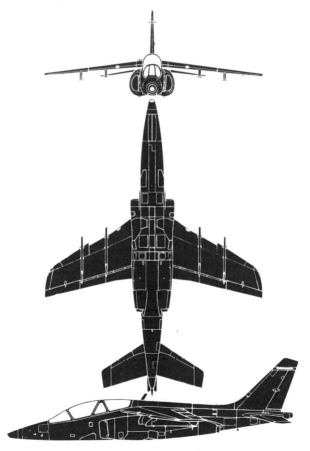

DE HAVILLAND CANADA DASH 7

Country of Origin: Canada.

Type: STOL regional airliner.

Power Plant: Four 1,120 shp Pratt & Whitney (Canada) PT6A-50 turboprops.

Performance: Max cruising speed (with 9,500-lb/4 309-kg payload of 50 passengers and baggage), 266 mph (428 km/h) at 8,000 ft (2 440 m); normal cruise, 262 mph (421 km/h) at 15,000 ft (4 570 m); range cruise, 248 mph (399 km/h); range (50 passengers and IFR reserves), 795 mls (1 280 km) at normal cruise, (with max fuel and 6,500-lb/2 948-kg payload), 1,347 mls (2 168 km).

Weights: Empty equipped, 27,600 lb (12 519 kg); max takeoff, 44,000 lb (19 958 kg).

Accommodation: Flight crew of two and standard seating for 50 passengers four-abreast with optional arrangement for 54 passengers or cargo/passenger mix.

Status: First of two pre-series aircraft flown 27 March 1975, with first production aircraft following on 30 May 1977. Production running at one monthly against airline orders for 89 aircraft at beginning of 1984.

Notes: Current basic aircraft is the Series 100, the all-cargo version being the Series 101, proposed versions including the Series 200 with 1,230 shp PT6A-55 engines and higher gross weights, and the Series 300 with a 19 ft 1¾ in (5,83 m) fuselage stretch to give a 78–84 seat maximum passenger capacity. The last-mentioned version will have PW115 engines of 1,500 shp. An example of a maritime surveillance version, the Dash 7R, has been supplied to the Canadian Coast Guard, and military operators of the Dash 7 are the Canadian Armed Forces (2) and the Venezuelan Navy (1). In Canadian military service the Dash 7 is designated CC-132.

DE HAVILLAND CANADA DASH 7

Dimensions: Span, 93 ft 0 in (28,35 m); length, 80 ft 7¾ in (24,58 m); height, 26 ft 2 in (7,98 m); wing area, 860 sq ft (79,90 m²).

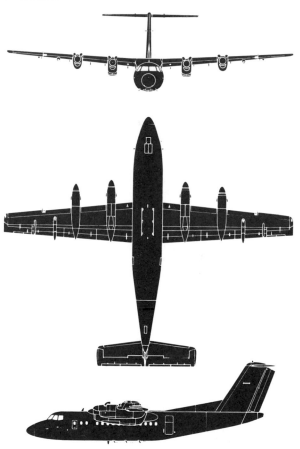

DE HAVILLAND CANADA DASH 8

Country of Origin: Canada.
Type: Regional airliner and corporate transport.
Power Plant: Two 2,000 shp Pratt & Whitney (Canada) PW120 turboprops.
Performance: Max cruise speed, 311 mph (500 km/h) at 15,000 ft (4 570 m), 301 mph (484 km/h) at 25,000 ft (7 620 m); max initial climb, 2,070 ft/min (10,51 m/sec); range (36 passengers and IFR reserves), 691 mls (1 112 km) at max cruise at 25,000 ft (7 620 m); max range (with 4,550-lb/2064 kg payload and max fuel), 1,493 mls (2 402 km).
Weights: Operational empty, 20,176 lb (9 152 kg); max take-off, 30,500 lb (13 835 kg).
Accommodation: Flight crew of two and standard arrangement for 36 passengers four-abreast with central aisle. Alternate arrangements for 37–39 passengers, mixed passenger-cargo operations and corporate executive transportation. Movable bulkhead to facilitate conversion to mixed-traffic or all-cargo configurations.
Status: The first of four pre-production prototypes was flown on 20 June 1983, with two more flown in October and November, and a fourth by beginning of 1984. Certification planned for autumn 1984, with first customer delivery (to NorOntair) in September 1984, four aircraft being delivered in that year, with 40 delivered in 1985 and a projected production tempo of six monthly in 1986. Orders for 53 aircraft placed by 15 operators by beginning of 1984 when a further 66 were on option.
Notes: The Dash 8 is an evolutionary design embodying service-proven features of the Dash 7 (see pages 84–85). The corporate version will feature an extended range capability, additional tankage permitting 2,590 miles (4 167 km) to be flown with a 1,200-lb (544-kg) payload at l-r cruise.

DE HAVILLAND CANADA DASH 8
Dimensions: Span, 85 ft 0 in (25,91 m); length, 73 ft 0 in (22,25 m); height, 25 ft 0 in (7,62 m); wing area, 585 sq ft (54,35 m²).

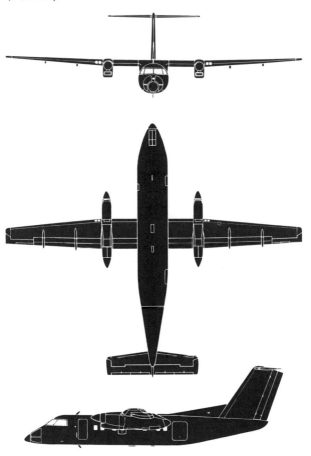

DORNIER DO 228

Country of Origin: Federal Germany.

Type: Light regional airliner and utility transport.

Power Plant: Two 715 shp Garrett AiResearch TPE 331-5 turboprops.

Performance: Max cruise speed, 268 mph (432 km/h) at 10,000 ft (3 280 m), 230 mph (370 km/h) at sea level; initial climb, 2,050 ft/min (10,4 m/sec); service ceiling, 29,600 ft (9 020 m); range (-100), 1,224 mls (1 970 km) at max range cruise, 1,075 mls (1 730 km) at max cruise, (-200), 715 mls (1 150 km) at max range cruise, 640 mls (1 030 km) at max cruise.

Weights: Operational empty (-100), 7,132 lb (3 235 kg), (-200), 7,450 lb (3 379 kg); max take-off, 12,570 lb (5 700 kg).

Accommodation: Flight crew of two and standard arrangements for (-100) 15 and (-200) 19 passengers in individual seats with central aisle.

Status: Prototype Do 228-100 flown on 28 March and -200 on 9 May 1981, and first customer delivery (A/S Norving) August 1982. Thirty-four Do 228s (both -100s and -200s) ordered by beginning of 1984 (plus 51 on option), in which year production is scheduled to run at two–three aircraft monthly.

Notes: The Do 228 mates a new-technology wing of super-critical section with the fuselage cross-section of the Do 128 (see 1982 edition), and two versions differing essentially in fuselage length and range capability are currently in production, the shorter-fuselage Do 228-100 and the longer-fuselage Do 228-200 (illustrated). All-cargo and corporate transport versions of the -100 are being offered, and geosurvey, maritime surveillance and military transport versions are proposed. The Do 228 has been selected by India to meet that country's LTA (Light Transport Aircraft) requirement. Ten are to be supplied by Dornier with approximately 140 to be built in India by HAL over a 10-year period.

DORNIER DO 228

Dimensions: Span, 55 ft 7 in (16,97 m); length (-100) 49 ft 3 in (15,03 m), (-200), 54 ft 3 in (16,55 m); height, 15 ft 9 in (4,86 m); wing area, 344·46 sq ft (32,00 m²).

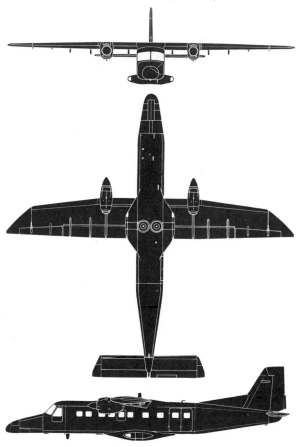

(CLAUDIUS) DORNIER SEASTAR

Country of Origin: Federal Germany.
Type: Light utility amphibious flying boat.
Power Plant: Two 500 shp Pratt & Whitney (Canada) PT6A-11 turboprops.
Performance: (Estimated) Max speed, 255 mph (410 km/h) at 6,560 ft (2 000 m); normal cruise, 200 mph (324 km/h) at 9,840 ft (3 000 m); initial climb (at 8,377 lb/3 800 kg), 1,770 ft/min (9,0 m/sec); range (with 3,000-lb/1 360-kg payload), 250 mls (402 km), (with 2,000-lb/907-kg payload), 545 mls (877 km).
Weights: Empty, 4,515 lb (2 048 kg); max take-off, 8,855 lb (4 017 kg).
Accommodation: Pilot and co-pilot/passenger side-by-side on flight deck and various arrangements for up to eight passengers in main cabin.
Status: The first prototype Seastar is scheduled to enter flight test during 1984, and current planning envisages delivery of the first series aircraft in 1986–87.
Notes: The Seastar has been developed by a team led by Prof Dipl-Ing Claudius Dornier (the project having no connection with Dornier GmbH) with the aim of meeting a requirement for a versatile light utility amphibian. Utilising glassfibre and carbonfibre composite construction to result in a corrosion-resistant hull, the Seastar is of centreline thrust concept with tandem-mounted engines and features a high-lift wing with fixed leading-edge slots and large-area trailing-edge flaps to achieve STOL capability. The Seastar will be capable of operation from grass, water, snow and ice, and will have a large upward-hinging freight loading door in the aft portside of the hull to facilitate its use in freight operations. A noteworthy feature of the design is its use of elongated sponsons.

(CLAUDIUS) DORNIER SEASTAR

Dimensions: Span, 48 ft 6⅔ in (14,80 m); length, 36 ft 5 in (11,10 m); height, 14 ft 5¼ in (4,40 m); wing area, 258·34 sq ft (24,00 m²).

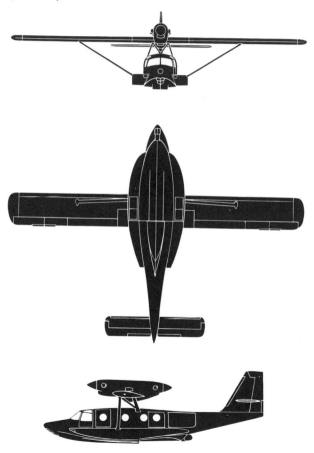

EDGLEY EA7 OPTICA

Country of Origin: United Kingdom.
Type: Three-seat observation aircraft.
Power Plant: One 200 hp Avco Lycoming IO-360 or 210 hp TIO-360 four-cylinder horizontally-opposed engine driving a ducted fan.
Performance: Max speed, 126 mph (203 km/h); cruise (65% power), 108 mph (174 km/h); loiter speed, 57 mph (92 km/h); initial climb, 720 ft/min (3,66 m/sec); service ceiling, 14,000 ft (4 270 m); range (65% power), 650 mls (1 050 km); max endurance at loiter speed, 10 hrs.
Weights: Empty, 1,875 lb (850 kg); max take-off, 2,725 lb (1 236 kg).
Status: Prototype flown on 14 December 1979. Initial order for 25 placed mid-1981, and preparations initiated for production of 60 Opticas annually with deliveries commencing 1984. The first pre-production Optica was completed in December 1983, and the first production aircraft was scheduled to follow in February 1984, when a production tempo of three monthly was expected to be attained, this rising to five monthly by year's end. Orders for more than 60 Opticas had been placed by the beginning of 1984.
Notes: Of unique concept, the Optica is intended primarily for pipeline and powerline inspection, traffic surveillance, forestry, coastal and frontier patrol, and aerial photography, tasks that it is claimed capable of performing at less than one-third of the initial and operating costs of a comparable helicopter normally utilised for such. The engine is part of a ducted propulsor unit which forms a power pod separate from the main shroud and mounted downstream of a five-bladed fixed-pitch fan. The Optica can take-off and clear 50 ft (15 m) within 655 ft (200 m) and land from 50 ft within 850 ft (260 m).

EDGLEY EA7 OPTICA

Dimensions: Span, 39 ft 4 in (12,00 m); length, 26 ft $9\frac{1}{4}$ in (8,16 m); height, 7 ft 7 in (2,31 m); wing area, 170·5 sq ft (15,84 m²).

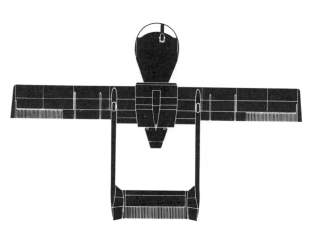

EMBRAER EMB-120 BRASILIA

Country of Origin: Brazil.

Type: Short-haul regional airliner.

Power Plant: Two 1,500 shp Pratt & Whitney (Canada) PW115 turboprops.

Performance: (At 21,165 lb/9 600 kg) Max cruise speed, 337 mph (542 km/h) at 20,000 ft (6 095 m); range cruise, 290 mph (467 km/h) at 20,000 ft (6 095 m); max climb, 2,650 ft/min (28,7 m/sec); service ceiling, 32000 ft (9 750 m); range (30 passengers and reserves), 628 mls (1 010 km); max range (14 passengers and reserves), 1,820 mls (2 930 km).

Weights: Empty equipped, 11,585 lb (5 255 kg); max take-off, 21,165 lb (9 600 kg).

Accommodation: Flight crew of two and optional arrangements for 24, 26 and 30 passengers three abreast with offset aisle.

Status: First prototype flown on 27 July 1983, with a further prototype scheduled to have entered flight test by the beginning of 1984, with Brazilian certification planned for August 1984 and US and European certification following in the last quarter of the year. Total of 107 options claimed at beginning of 1984, including 24 for the Brazilian Air Force and two for the Chilean Air Force. First customer deliveries scheduled for early 1985, with production of three aircraft monthly to be attained in that year, increasing to four monthly in 1986.

Notes: Variants of the Brasilia being actively pursued at the beginning of 1984 included a corporate executive transport and a maritime surveillance and ASW aircraft. A 36-passenger "stretched" version is a longer-term project.

EMBRAER EMB-120 BRASILIA

Dimensions: Span, 64 ft 10¾ in (19,78 m); length, 65 ft 7 in (20,00 m); height, 20 ft 10 in (6,35 m); wing area, 409·3 sq ft (38,03 m²).

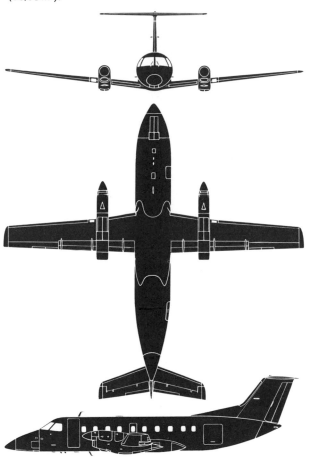

EMBRAER EMB-312 (T-27) TUCANO

Country of Origin: Brazil.

Type: Tandem two-seat basic and weapons trainer.

Power Plant: One 750 shp Pratt & Whitney (Canada) PT6A-25C turboprop.

Performance: (At 5,622 lb/2 550 kg) Max speed, 270 mph (435 km/h) at 10,000 ft (3 050 m); econ cruise, 199 mph (320 km/h) at 10,000 ft (3 050 m); initial climb, 2,590 ft/min (13,15 m/sec); service ceiling, 28,500 ft (8 685 m); range (internal fuel), 1,180 mls (1 897 km).

Weights: Empty equipped, 3,487 lb (1 582 kg); max take-off (aerobatic), 5,622 lb (2 550 kg), (with external stores), 7,000 lb (3 175 kg).

Armament: (Weapons training and light strike) Four underwing stations for total ordnance load of 1,323 lb (600 kg) which may comprise two 0·5-in (12,7-mm) gun pods, four pods each with seven 37-mm or 70-mm rockets, or four 250-lb (113-kg) bombs.

Status: First of four prototypes flown on 15 August 1980, with deliveries against Brazilian Air Force order for 118 aircraft (plus option on further 50) commencing 29 September 1983. Production rate of seven-eight monthly attained by beginning of 1984. Ten are to be delivered in December 1984 to Egypt where a further 110 are to be built, initially from component sets.

Notes: The Tucano (Toucan) is unique among current production turboprop trainers in not having been derived from an earlier piston-engined design and in having ejection seats. It is intended to simulate the flying characteristics of a pure jet aircraft which can thus be ommitted from the basic wings syllabus of the Brazilian Air Force. The Tucano is initially replacing the Cessna T-37 pure jet trainer in Brazilian service.

EMBRAER EMB-312 (T-27) TUCANO

Dimensions: Span, 36 ft 6½ in (11,14 m); length, 32 ft 4¼ in (9,86 m); height, 11 ft 1⅞ in (3,40 m); wing area, 208·82 sq ft (19,40 m²).

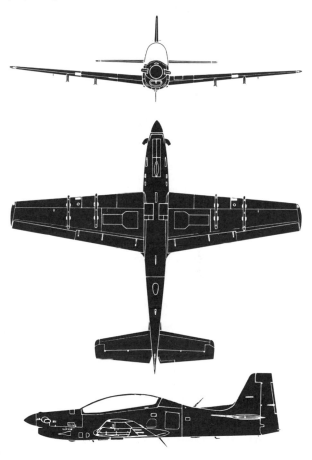

FAIRCHILD 300

Country of Origin: USA.

Type: Light corporate executive transport.

Power Plant: Two 900 shp Garrett TPE-331-10U-503G turboprops.

Performance: (At 10,000 lb/4 536 kg) Max cruise speed, 341 mph (549 km/h) at 10,000 ft (3 050 m), 345 mph (556 km/h) at 20,000 ft (6 095 m); initial climb (at 13,230 lb/6 001 kg), 2,600 ft/min (13,21 m/sec); service ceiling, 27,400 ft (8 350 m); max range (at max cruise at 28,000 ft/8 535 m with 45 min reserve), 2,508 mls (4 036 km) with two crew, 2,249 mls (3 458 km) with six occupants, 1,619 mls (2 605 km) with 10 occupants.

Weights: Empty, 8,200 lb (3 719 kg); max take-off, 13,230 lb (6 001 kg).

Accommodation: Pilot and co-pilot/passenger on flight deck and various arrangements 7–10 passengers in main cabin.

Status: A progressive development of the Swearingen Merlin IIIC, the Fairchild 300 entered flight test early May 1983, and initial customer deliveries were scheduled to commence late 1984.

Notes: The Fairchild 300 is the latest production version of the Merlin series of twin-turboprop pressurised executive transport aircraft originally developed by the Swearingen Aviation Corporation which became a wholly-owned subsidiary of Fairchild Industries in 1979. By comparison with the Merlin IIIC (introduced in 1981), the Fairchild 400 introduces winglets to reduce spanwise airflow, new ailerons and various refinements, these changes resulting in improved speed, climb and landing performance, and better handling characteristics.

FAIRCHILD 300

Dimensions: Span, 47 ft 10⅜ in (16,60 m); length, 42 ft 2⅝ in (12,86 m); height, 16 ft 9½ in (5,12 m).

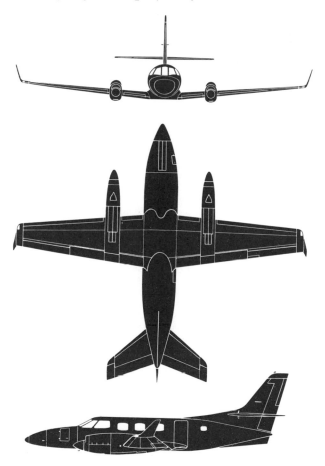

FAIRCHILD 400

Country of Origin: USA.
Type: Light corporate executive transport.
Power Plant: Two 1,100 shp Garrett TPE-331-14UA/UB-80IG turboprops.
Performance: Max cruise speed, 397 mph (639 km/h) at 15,000 ft (4 570 m), 400 mph (643 km/h) at 20,000 ft (6 095 m), 364 mph (586 km/h) at 35,000 ft (10 670 m); initial climb, 2,353 ft/min (11,95 m/sec); service ceiling, 33,090 ft (10 085 m); range at 388 mph (625 km/h) at 30,000 ft (9 145 m) with 45 min reserve, 1,944 mls (3 128 km) with two crew, 1,832 mls (2 948 km) with 9 occupants, 1,402 mls (2 255 km) with 16 occupants.
Weights: Empty, 9,686 lb (4 394 kg): max take-off, 16,500 lb (7 484 kg).
Accommodation: Crew of two on flight deck and various arrangements in main cabin for 7–14 passengers.
Status: A derivative of the Merlin IVC (now known as the Farichild IVC), the Fairchild 400 entered flight test during the first half of 1983, and is scheduled for certification in 1985, at which time customer deliveries will commence.
Notes: Externally similar to the Fairchild IVC (formerly Merlin IVC), the Fairchild 400 introduces uprated engines which, at 20,000 ft (6 095 m), develop some 70 per cent more power than the TPE-331-11U-601G engines of the earlier aircraft, new ailerons and control linkage, and various more minor refinements. The Fairchild IVC offers similar accommodation in the business executive transport role, but may be rapidly converted to cargo configuration or to a combination of passengers and cargo. An optimised all-cargo version of the basic design is known as the Expediter and a regional transport version is designated Metro III.

FAIRCHILD 400

Dimensions: Span, 57 ft 0 in (17,37 m); length, 59 ft 4¼ in (18,09 m); height, 16 ft 8 in (5,08 m); wing area, 309 sq ft (28,71 m²).

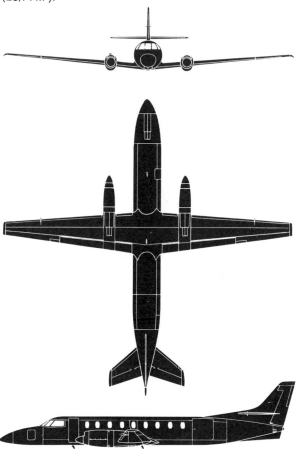

FMA IA 63

Country of Origin: Argentina.

Type: Tandem two-seat basic and advanced trainer.

Power Plant: One 3,500 lb st (1 588 kgp) Garrett TFE731-2N turbofan.

Performance: (Estimated at 7,055 lb/3 200 kg) Max speed, 460 mph (740 km/h) at sea level; initial climb, 5,315 ft/min (27 m/sec); service ceiling, 42,325 ft (12 900 m); range (max internal fuel), 930 mls (1 500 km) at 345 mph (560 km/h) at 13,125 ft (4 000 m).

Weights: Normal loaded (flying training mission), 7,716 lb (3 500 kg); max take-off (armament training and light attack), 10,250 lb (4 650 kg).

Status: The first of four flying prototypes is scheduled to enter test in April 1984, and current planning envisages production deliveries (against Argentine Air Force requirement for 100 aircraft) commencing mid-1986, with peak production rate of three aircraft monthly. First series IA 63 scheduled to fly at the end of 1985, and 22 aircraft will be built during 1986-87.

at the end of 1985, and 22 aircraft will be built during 1986-87.

Notes: The IA 63 has been developed by the Federal German Dornier concern under contract to the Fabrica Militar de Aviones (FMA) as a technology transfer programme, the project having been progressively transferred to the FMA's Cordoba facilities, the entire programme becoming an FMA responsibility with the initiation of flight testing. Dornier is now acting only in an advisory capacity in the programme. The IA 63 is expected to enter service with the *Escuela Aviación Militar* from February 1988, and it is anticipated that an optimised light strike version will be developed.

FMA IA 63

Dimensions: Span, 31 ft 9⅓ in (9,69 m); length, 35 ft 10¼ in (10,93 m) height, 14 ft 0¾ in (4,29 m); wing area, 168·24 sq ft (15,63 m²).

FOKKER F28 FELLOWSHIP MK 4000

Country of Origin: Netherlands.

Type: Short/medium-haul commercial airliner.

Power Plant: Two 9,850 lb st (4 468 kgp) Rolls-Royce RB. 183-2 Spey Mk 555-15H turbofans.

Performance: Max cruising speed, 523 mph (843 km/h) at 23,000 ft (7 000 m); econ cruise, 487 mph (783 km/h) at 32,000 ft (9 755 m); range cruise, 421 mph (678 km/h) at 30,000 ft (9 145 m); range (with max payload), 1,160 mls (1 870 km), (with max fuel), 2,566 mls (4 130 km); cruise altitude, 35,000 ft (10 675 m).

Weights: Operational empty, 38,825 lb (17 661 kg); max take-off, 73,000 lb (33 110 kg).

Accommodation: Flight crew of two (with jump seat for optional third crew member) and basic main cabin single-class configuration for 85 passengers five-abreast.

Status: First of two F28 prototypes flown on 8 May 1967, with first customer delivery following on 24 February 1969. Total of 207 ordered by beginning of 1984, with 194 delivered and production running at 1·5 monthly.

Notes: The F28 Mk 4000, which first flew in October 1976, provides the bulk of current production, the Mks 3000 and 4000 having supplanted the Mks 1000 and 2000 (after completion of 97 and 10 respectively). Whereas the Mk 3000 has the 80 ft 6½ in (24,55 m) fuselage of the Mk 1000, offering seating for up to 65 passengers, the Mk 4000 has the lengthened fuselage introduced by the Mk 2000. Both versions have the extended wing originally developed for the (subsequently discarded) Mks 5000 and 6000. At the beginning of 1984, work was continuing on a major update of the F28, the Fokker 100, with the new 13,500 lb st (6 146 kgp) Rolls-Royce Tay turbofans, a revised wing and a fuselage "stretch" to permit accommodation of 107–109 passengers.

FOKKER F28 FELLOWSHIP MK 4000

Dimensions: Span, 82 ft 3 in (25,07 m); length, 97 ft 1¾ in (29,61 m); height, 27 ft 9½ in (8,47 m); wing area, 850 sq ft (78,97 m²).

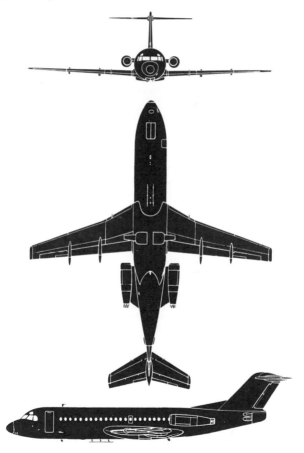

GATES LEARJET MODEL 55

Country of Origin: USA.
Type: Light corporate executive transport.
Power Plant: Two 3,700 lb st (1 678 kgp) Garrett TFE 731-3A-2B turbofans.
Performance: Max cruising speed, 525 mph (845 km/h) at 41,000 ft (12 495 m); time to 41,000 ft (12 495 m), 24 min; max. altitude, 51,000 ft (15 545 m); range (four passengers and 45 min reserves), 2,666 mls (4 290 km), (with 2,000 lb/907 kg payload), 2,073 mls (3 335 km).
Weights: Typical empty equipped, 12,600 lb (5 715 kg); max take-off, 19,500 lb (8 845 kg), (optional), 20,500 lb (9 299 kg).
Accommodation: Flight crew of two and various main cabin arrangements for up to a maximum of 11 passengers. Typical arrangements include five individual seats and a bench-type seat for two, and four individual seats and a bench-type seat for four.
Status: The first of two prototypes flew on 19 April 1979, with first production aircraft following on 11 August 1980. Customer deliveries commenced 30 April 1981, some 85 having been delivered by beginning of 1984.
Notes: Originally known as the Longhorn, the Model 55 is available in extended-range 55ER, 55LR and 55XLR versions, fuel tankage replacing the tail baggage compartment and, in the case of the special-mission 55XLR, an aft cabin tank being provided to boost range to 3,340 mls (5 375 km).

GATES LEARJET MODEL 55

Dimensions: Span, 43 ft 9½ in (13,34 m); length, 55 ft 1½ in (16,79 m); height, 14 ft 8 in (4,47 m); wing area, 264·5 sq ft (24,57 m²).

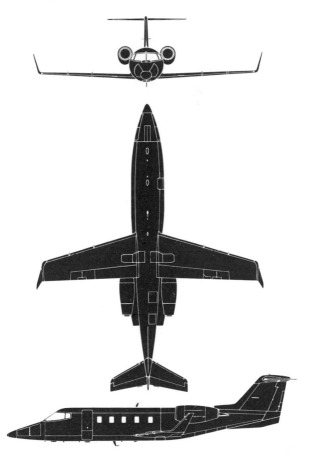

GENERAL DYNAMICS F-16 FIGHTING FALCON

Country of Origin: USA.

Type: (F-16A) Single-seat multi-role fighter and (F-16B) two-seat operational trainer.

Power Plant: One 14,800 lb st (6 713 kgp) dry and 23,830 lb st (10 809 kgp) reheat Pratt & Whitney F100-PW-200 turbofan.

Performance: Max speed (short endurance dash), 1,333 mph (2 145 km/h) or Mach 2·02, (sustained), 1,247 mph (2 007 km/h) or Mach 1·89 at 40,000 ft (12 190 m); max. cruise, 614 mph (988 km/h) or Mach 0·93; tactical radius (HI-LO-HI interdiction on internal fuel), 360 mls (580 km) with six 500-lb (227-kg) bombs; range (similar ordnance load and internal fuel), 1,200 mls (1 930 km) at 575 mph (925 km/h).

Weights: Operational empty, 14,567 lb (6 613 kg); max take-off, 35,400 lb (16 057 kg).

Armament: One 20-mm M61A-1 multi-barrel rotary cannon and from two to six AIM-9L/M AAMs, or (air support) up to 12,000 lb (5 443 kg) of ordnance between nine stations.

Status: First of two (YF-16) prototypes flown 20 January 1974. First production F-16 flown 7 August 1978, with some 1,090 delivered by 1983 by parent company (10 monthly) and European consortium (five monthly), the latter having final assembly lines in Belgium and Netherlands. USAF procurement calls for 2,165 F-16s. European programme embraces 160 for Belgium, 58 for Denmark, 213 for Netherlands and 96 for Norway. Export orders comprise Israel (150), Egypt (80), Pakistan (40), South Korea (36) and Venezuela (24). In addition, Turkey is expected to co-produce 160 F-16s.

Notes: Single-seat F-16C and two-seat F-16D with upgraded systems to be delivered from July 1984. The 1,000th F-16 was rolled out on 8 July 1983.

GENERAL DYNAMICS F-16 FIGHTING FALCON

Dimensions: Span (excluding missiles), 31 ft 0 in (9,45 m); length, 47 ft 7¾ in (14,52 m); height, 16 ft 5¼ in (5,01 m); wing area, 300 sq ft (27,87 m²).

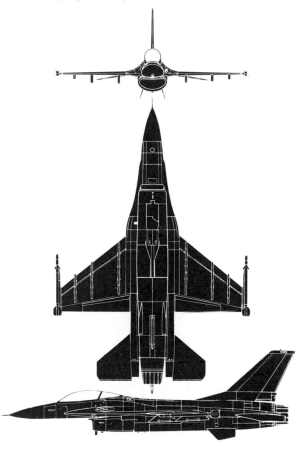

GRUMMAN E-2C HAWKEYE

Country of Origin: USA.
Type: Airborne early warning, surface surveillance and strike control aircraft.
Power Plant: Two 4,910 ehp Allison T56-A-425 turboprops.
Performance: Max speed, 348 mph (560 km/h) at 10,000 ft (3 050 m); max range cruise, 309 mph (498 km/h); initial climb, 2,515 ft/min (12,8 m/sec); service ceiling, 30,800 ft (9 390 m); mission endurance (at 230 mls/370 km from base), 4·0 hrs; max endurance, 6·1 hrs; ferry range, 1,604 mls (2 580 km).
Weights: Empty, 38,009 lb (17 240 kg); max take-off, 51,900 lb (23 540 kg).
Accommodation: Crew of five comprising flight crew of two and Airborne Tactical Data System team of three, each occupying an independent operating station.
Status: First of two E-2C prototypes flown on 20 January 1971, with first production aircraft flying on 23 September 1972. Total US Navy requirement for 101 by 1986. Four delivered to Israel, and first four of eight ordered by Japan delivered in 1983. First of two E-2Cs for Egypt expected to be delivered during 1985.
Notes: The E-2C is the current production version of the Hawkeye, having followed 59 E-2As (all subsequently updated to E-2B standards), and is able to operate independently, in co-operation with other aircraft, or in concert with a ground environment. Two have been delivered to the US Navy as TE-2Cs for use as conversion trainers by the Service's two Hawkeye readiness squadrons which support 12 four-aircraft Hawkeye squadrons attached to the carrier air wings.

GRUMMAN E-2C HAWKEYE

Dimensions: Span, 80 ft 7 in (24,56 m); length, 57 ft 7 in (17,55 m); height, 18 ft 4 in (5,69 m); wing area, 700 sq ft (65,03 m²).

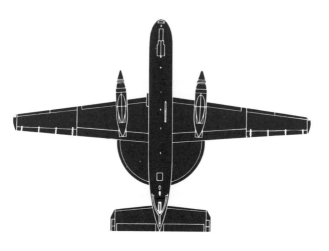

GRUMMAN F-14A TOMCAT

Country of Origin: USA.

Type: Two-seat shipboard multi-role fighter.

Power Plant: Two 12,500 lb st (5 670 kgp) dry and 20,900 lb st (9 840 kgp) reheat Pratt & Whitney TF30-P-412A or P-414 turbofans.

Performance: Max speed (with four semi-recessed AIM-7 AAMs), 913 mph (1 470 km/h) or Mach 1·2 at sea level, 1,584 mph (2 549 km/h) or Mach 2·4 at 49,000 ft (14 935 m); time to 60,000 ft (18 290 m) at 55,000 lb (24 948 kg), 2·1 min; tactical radius (combat air patrol on internal fuel), 765 mls (1 232 km).

Weights: Empty, 39,930 lb (18 112 kg); loaded (intercept mission with four AIM-7s), 58,904 lb (26 718 kg), (with six AIM-54s), 69,790 lb (31 656 kg); max take-off, 74,348 lb (33 724 kg).

Armament: One 20-mm M61A-1 rotary cannon and (intercept) six AIM-7E/F Sparrow and four AIM-9G/H Sidewinder AAMs, or six AIM-54A Phoenix and two AIM-9G/H AAMs.

Status: First of 12 research and development aircraft flown 21 December 1970, with 480 delivered to US Navy by beginning of 1984, when production was expected to continue at a rate of 30 annually through Fiscal 1994 for an eventual total of 845 aircraft. Forty-nine being delivered as RF-14As for photo-recce role.

Notes: An engine upgrading programme (commencing with new aircraft), together with avionics and radar improvement programmes scheduled to commence 1985. Re-engining F-14s with either General Electric F110 or Pratt & Whitney PW1130 turbofans remains an option.

GRUMMAN F-14A TOMCAT

Dimensions: Span (20 deg sweep), 64 ft 1½ in (19,55 m); (68 deg sweep), 37 ft 7 in (11,45 m); length, 61 ft 11⅞ in (18,90 m); height, 16 ft 0 in (4,88 m); wing area, 565 sq ft (52,50 m²).

GRUMMAN X-29A

Country of Origin: USA.

Type: Single-seat advanced technology demonstration aircraft.

Power Plant: One 10,600 lb st (4 810 kgp) dry and 15,800 lb st (7 167 kgp) reheat General Electric F404-GE-400 turbofan.

Performance: Estimated max speed, 1,056 mph (1 700 km/h) or Mach 1·6 above 36,000 ft (10 975 m).

Weights: Empty, 13,400 lb (6 078 kg); max take-off, 17,400 lb (7 893 kg).

Status: First of two examples to enter flight test April 1984.

Notes: The X-29A has been developed to demonstrate the benefits of forward wing sweep and features a digital fly-by-wire system and a thin supercritical wing largely of graphite composite construction with a variable-camber trailing edge mated with all-moving foreplanes (or canard surfaces). Up to 57 per cent of the X-29A comprises off-the-shelf components to reduce costs, these including a Northrop F-5A front fuselage and a flight control system and undercarrriage from the General Dynamics F-16A. Forward wing sweep is believed to be particularly applicable to tactical fighter aircraft, offering, by comparison with conventional sweptback wings, higher manœuvrability, improved low-speed handling and lower stalling speeds. Data accumulated from X-29A testing will be fed into the USAF's Advanced Tactical Fighter Program.

GRUMMAN X-29A

Dimensions: Span, 27 ft 0 in (8,23 m); length, 48 ft 0 in (14,63 m); height, 14 ft 0 in (4,27 m); wing area, 188·84 sq ft (17,54 m²).

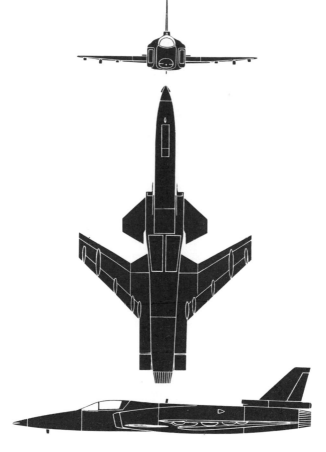

GULFSTREAM AEROSPACE COMMANDER JETPROP 1000

Country of Origin: USA.

Type: Light corporate executive transport.

Power Plant: Two 820 shp Garrett TPE 331-10-501K turbo-props.

Performance: Max cruise speed, 355 mph (571 km/h) at 22,000 ft (6 700 m); econ cruise, 295 mph (474 km/h) at 35,000 ft (10 670 m); max initial climb, 2,800 ft/min (14,22 m/sec); range with 45 min reserves (max payload), 1,510 mls (2 429 km), (max fuel), 2,395 mls (3 855 km).

Weights: Empty equipped, 7,210 lb (3 270 kg); max take-off, 11,200 lb (5 080 kg).

Accommodation: Pilot and co-pilot/passenger side-by-side and standard layout for six passengers. Maximum seating for 11 passengers.

Status: A progressive development of earlier Commander Jet-props (the 840, 900 and 980), the Commander Jetprop 1000 flew on 12 May 1980, production deliveries commencing in July 1981, and a multi-mission version being introduced in May 1983.

Notes: The Commander Jetprop 1000 is currently the latest production version of the series to which will be added the 1200 early in 1985, this last-mentioned model, flown as a prototype in August 1983, featuring uprated engines with which it achieves a max cruise close to 400 mph (644 km/h). All have the same overall external dimensions, but the 1000 has increased cabin volume as a result of rearward shift of the aft pressure bulkhead. The multi-mission version of the 1000 introduced in 1983 can be rapidly converted from executive trans-port to cargo or medevac configurations and introduces a new cargo door.

GULFSTREAM AEROSPACE COMMANDER JETPROP 1000

Dimensions: Span, 52 ft 1½ in (15,89 m); length, 42 ft 11¾ in (13,10 m); height, 14 ft 11½ in (4,55 m); wing area, 279·37 sq ft (25,95 m²).

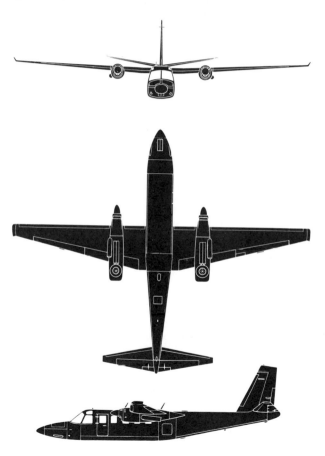

GULFSTREAM AEROSPACE GULFSTREAM III

Country of Origin: USA.
Type: Corporate transport and (SMA-3) multi-mission aircraft.
Power Plant: Two 11,400 lb st (5171 kgp) Rolls-Royce RB.163–25 Spey Mk 511-8 turbofans.
Performance: Max cruising speed, 577 mph (928 km/h) or Mach 0·85 at 30,000 ft (9145 m); long-range cruise, 512 mph (825 km/h) or Mach 0·775; initial climb, 3,800 ft/min (19,3 m/sec); max operating altitude, 45,000 ft (13 715 m); range (VFR reserves and 1,600 lb/726 kg payload), 4,720 mls (7 595 km), (IFR reserves), 4,200 mls (6 760 km).
Weights: Manufacturer's bare empty, 36,346 lb (16 486 kg); max take-off, 68,200 lb (30 936 kg).
Accommodation: (SMA-3) Flight crew of two or three and (personnel transport) up to 19 passengers or (medical evacuation) 15 litter patients and two medical attendants. For maritime surveillance a flight crew of three and three systems operators are carried, and in the cargo role up to 4,630 lb (2 100 kg) may be carried.
Status: Three Gulfstream SMA-3s were delivered to the Royal Danish Air Force during 1982, this service having an option on two further aircraft. The SMA-3 is a multi-mission version of the Gulfstream III corporate executive transport first flown on 2 December 1979. Customer deliveries commenced in September 1980, and some 100 delivered by beginning of 1984.
Notes: The Gulfstream SMA-3 (illustrated on opposite page) differs from the basic Gulfstream III primarily in having a large freight door in the starboard side and APS-127 surveillance radar. The first of 11 Gulfstream IIIs leased (but eventually to be purchased) to the USAF as C-20As were delivered in September 1983.

GULFSTREAM AEROSPACE GULFSTREAM III

Dimensions: Span, 77 ft 10 in (23,72 m); length 83 ft 1 in (25,30 m); height, 24 ft 4½ in (7,40 m); wing area, 934·6 sq ft (86,82 m²).

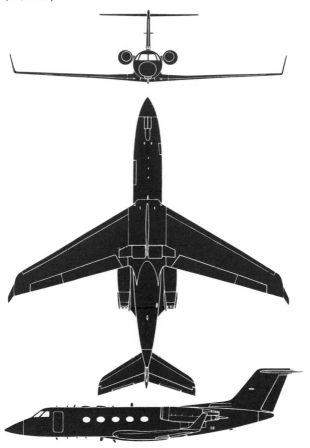

GULFSTREAM AEROSPACE PEREGRINE

Country of Origin: USA.

Type: Light corporate transport.

Power Plant: One 2,900 lb st (1 316 kgp) Pratt & Whitney JT15D-5 turbofan.

Performance: Max speed, 416 mph (669 km/h) at 31,000 ft (9 450 m); max cruise, 381 mph (613 km/h) at 35,000 ft (10 670 m); initial climb, 2,877 ft/min (14,6 m/sec); service ceiling, 38,400 ft (11 705 m); max range (with 45 min reserves), 1,600 mls (2 574 km); max payload range, 1,150 mls (1 850 km).

Weights: Empty, 5,120 lb (2 322 kg); max take-off, 8,800 lb (3 992 kg).

Accommodation: Pilot and co-pilot/passenger on flight deck and provision for four-six passengers in main cabin.

Status: Prototype flown on 14 January 1983. At beginning of 1984, orders for 50 aircraft were considered a prerequisite to a three-year development programme for the proposed series production version (described above), with certification in 1986.

Notes: The Peregrine corporate transport, initially known as the Commander Fanjet 1500, is closely related to the Peregrine side-by-side two-seat basic trainer (see 1982 edition), possessing some component commonality. The be certificated for single-pilot operation, the Peregrine is the only aircraft in its category to be powered by a single engine. The prototype is powered by a 2,200 lb st (1 000 kgp) JT15D-1 turbofan which is to be replaced by the more powered -5 engine in the series version, but a twin-engined version is also envisaged. It is also proposed that the production model will have a 5-in (12,7-cm) increase in fuselage width. The Peregrine is aimed particularly at the business manager that flies his own aircraft.

GULFSTREAM AEROSPACE PEREGRINE

Dimensions: Span, 39 ft 2 in (11,94 m); length, 42 ft 1½ in (12,84 m); height, 16 ft 11¾ in (5,17 m).

IAI 1125 WESTWIND ASTRA

Country of Origin: Israel.

Type: Light corporate transport.

Power Plant: Two 3,650 lb st (1 656 kgp) Garrett TFE731-3B-100G turbofans.

Performance: Max cruising speed, 545 mph (877 km/h) at 35,000 ft (10 670 m); long-range cruise, 475 mph (765 km/h); max altitude, 45,000 ft (13 715 m); range (max fuel and five passengers) at high-speed cruise, 3,070 ml (4 938 km), at long-range cruise, 3,842 mls (6 184 km).

Weights: Basic operational (typical), 12,670 lb (5 747 kg); max take-off, 23,500 lb (10 660 kg).

Accommodation: Flight crew of two and standard main cabin arrangement for six passengers.

Status: First of two prototypes rolled out on 1 September 1983, and scheduled to enter flight test March 1984. The first batch of six Astras planned to be ready for delivery to customers by October 1985, with delivery rate attaining three monthly by March 1986.

Notes: The Astra retains the fuselage of the Model 1124 Westwind II embodying some design refinement and mated with a new and relocated high-speed swept wing. Except for the tail assembly and engine nacelles, which are nearly identical with those of the Westwind II, the Astra requires all new tooling, and some four per cent of the Astra by weight is made of composite materials. By comparison with that of the earlier aircraft, the fuselage of the Astra is 40 in (102 cm) longer and offers 8 in (20 cm) more cabin headroom as a result of reshaping the frames and the adoption of a low- rather than mid-positioned wing, the reshaped frames also offering a 2-in (5-cm) increase in cabin width. Provision is made for two 41·6 Imp gal (190 l) auxiliary tanks in the baggage compartment.

IAI 1125 WESTWIND ASTRA

Dimensions: Span, 52 ft 8 in (16,05 m); length, 55 ft 7 in (16,94 m); height, 18 ft 2 in (5,53 m); wing area, 316·6 sq ft (29,41 m²).

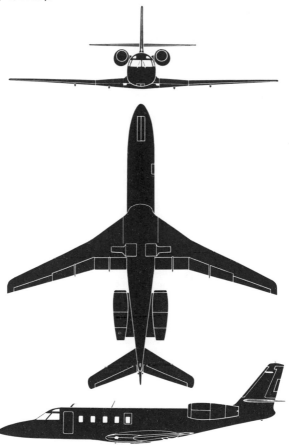

ICA IAR-831 PELICAN

Country of Origin: Romania.

Type: Tandem two-seat basic trainer.

Power Plant: One 290 hp Avco Lycoming IO-540-GID5 six-cylinder horizontally-opposed engine.

Performance: Max speed, 199 mph (320 km/h); cruising speed (75% power), 183 mph (295 km/h); initial climb, 1,380 ft/min (7,0 m/sec); ceiling, 18,370 ft (5 600 m); max range, 810 mls (1 300 km).

Weights: Max take-off (aerobatic), 2,645 lb (1 200 kg), (utility), 3,040 lb (1 380 kg), (normal category), 3,310 lb (1 500 kg).

Status: Prototype flight testing initiated 1982–83. No details of production plans available at the time of closing for press.

Notes: The IAR-831 Pelican reverses the usual trend in that it is a piston-engined version of the IAR-825TP Triumf (see 1983 edition) turboprop-powered basic trainer, although it may be assumed that both aircraft were developed in parallel. Both aircraft are described by ICA as having been designed to the EMRTA concept for an economical multi-role training aircraft, able to offer jet flying characteristics with classic aircraft costs. The airframes of the Pelican and Triumf appear fundamentally identical apart from changes associated with the type of power plant installed, the installation of a piston engine in the former, for example, resulting in a shorter nose. It is possible that the Pelican is intended as a successor to the similarly-powered IAR-823 in part of the Romanian Air Force's flying training syllabus, leading on to the turboprop-powered Triumf. It is also to be offered for export outside the Comecon organisation.

ICA IAR-831 PELICAN

Dimensions: Span, 32 ft 9½ in (10,00 m); length, 29 ft 2¼ in (8,90 m); height, 7 ft 9½ in (2,38 m); wing area, 161·5 sq ft (15,00 m²).

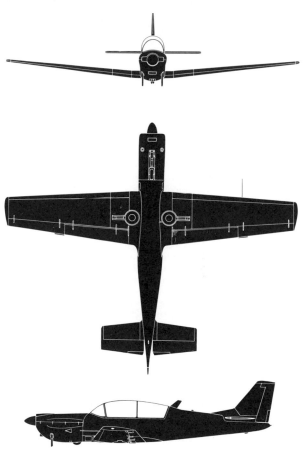

ILYUSHIN (MAINSTAY)

Country of Origin: USSR.
Type: Airborne warning and control system aircraft.
Power Plant: Four 26,455 lb st (12 000 kgp) Solovien D-30KP turbofans.
Performance: (Estimated) Max cruise speed, 475 mph (764 km/h) at 29,500-42,650 ft (9 000-13 000 m); loiter speed, 390-410 mph (630-660 km/h) at 29,500 ft (9 000 m); time on station (unrefuelled) at 930 mls (1 500 km) from base, 6-7 hrs.
Weights: (Estimated) Max take-off, 380,000 lb (172 370 kg).
Accommodation: Probable flight crew of four with tactical and air direction teams totalling 9-10 personnel.
Status: Mainstay has been derived from the Il-76 freighter and is known to have been under test since 1979-80. It is anticipated that Mainstay will attain initial operational status during 1984, and that some 30 will be in service by 1986-7.
Notes: A derivative of the Il-76 (see 1983 edition), Mainstay is believed to differ from the freighter primarily in having an over-fuselage "saucer" rotating radome with AWACS avionics in the main cabin, some nominal lengthening of the forward fuselage and provision for flight refuelling. Mainstay is intended to replace the Tu-126 Moss which possessed only limited capability over land, and will be used to vector interceptors with lookdown/shootdown capability towards low-level penetrating aircraft. The Foxhound (see pages 152-3) is apparently optimised for operation with Mainstay. Production of the Il-76 transport for both military and commercial use was continuing at the beginning of 1984 at approximately 35-40 annually, with some 185-200 delivered. It may be assumed that Mainstay is being produced on the same assembly line as the transport.

ILYUSHIN (MAINSTAY)

Dimensions: (Estimated) Span, 165 ft 8⅓ in (50,50 m); length, 155 ft 9 in (47,50 m); height, 48 ft 5 in (14,76 m); wing area, 3,299·2 sq ft (300,00 m²).

ILYUSHIN IL-86 (CAMBER)

Country of Origin: USSR.

Type: Medium-haul commercial airliner.

Power Plant: Four 28,660lb st (13 000 kgp) Kuznetsov NK-86 turbofans.

Performance: Max cruising speed, 590 mph (950 km/h) at 29,530 ft (9 000 m); econ cruise, 559 mph (900 km/h) at 36,090 ft (11 000 m); range (with max payload—350 passengers), 2,485 mls (4 000 km), (with 250 passengers), 3,107 mls (5 000 km).

Weights: Max take-off, 454,150 lb (206 000 kg).

Accommodation: Basic flight crew of three-four and up to 350 passengers nine-abreast with two aisles and divided between three cabins seating 111, 141 and 98 passengers.

Status: First prototype flown on 22 December 1976, and production prototype flown on 24 October 1977. Deliveries to Aeroflot commenced 1980, and some 25 are believed to have been delivered by the beginning of 1984. The Polish WSK-Mielec concern is responsible for manufacture of the entire wing, stabiliser and engine pylons. Four Il-86s are scheduled to be delivered to Polish Airlines LOT.

Notes: The Il-86 operated its first scheduled service (Moscow–Tashkent) on 26 December 1980, and first international service (Moscow–Prague) on 12 October 1981, but there has been an unexplained slippage in Aeroflot's programmed introduction of the Il-86 on many routes and it is believed that performance has fallen short of expectations. It is expected that production will be restricted in favour of the longer-range derivative type, the Il-96, which it is anticipated will be powered by the new D-18T turbofan in the 50,700 lb st (23 000 kgp) category. Sub-assemblies for the Il-96 are to be manufactured by the WSK-Mielec in Poland under a collaborative agreement, and this intended successor to the Il-86 is scheduled to enter service in the late 'eighties.

ILYUSHIN IL-86 (CAMBER)

Dimensions: Span, 157 ft 8⅛ in (48,06 m); length, 195 ft 4 in (59,54 m); height, 51 ft 10½ in (15,81 m); wing area, 3,550 sq ft (329,80 m²).

LEAR FAN 2100

Country of Origin: USA.
Type: Light corporate executive transport.
Power Plant: Two 650 shp Pratt & Whitney (Canada) PT6B-35F turboshafts.
Performance: (Estimated) Max speed, 414 mph (667 km/h) at 20,000 ft (6 095 m); range cruise, 345 mph (556 km/h); initial climb, 3,450 ft/min (17,53 m/sec); service ceiling, 41,000 ft (12 495 m); max range, 1,900 mls (3 058 km) at 345 mph (556 km/h).
Weights: Empty, 4,100 lb (1 860 kg); max take-off, 7,350 lb (3 334 kg).
Accommodation: Pilot and co-pilot/passenger on flight deck and various arrangements for up to eight passengers in main cabin.
Status: Two prototypes flown on 1 January 1981 and 18 June 1982 respectively, with first production configuration aircraft following September 1983. Certification planned for March 1984, with first customer deliveries following from autumn 1984. Lear Fan 2100 to be built at Aldergrove, Belfast, the components of the first 42 being shipped to Reno, Nevada, for final assembly, the 43rd and subsequent aircraft being assembled in Northern Ireland and flown to Reno for completion and outfitting. Orders for more than 200 aircraft were claimed at the beginning of 1984, when it was anticipated that production tempo will reach 12 monthly in 1986.
Notes: Featuring both radical structure and power system, the Lear Fan 2100 is manufactured primarily of composite materials and the turboshafts drive a pusher propeller via a gearbox drive train.

LEAR FAN 2100

Dimensions: Span, 39 ft 4 in (11,99 m); length, 40 ft 7 in (12,37 m); height, 12 ft 2 in (3,70 m); wing area, 162·9 sq ft (15,13 m²).

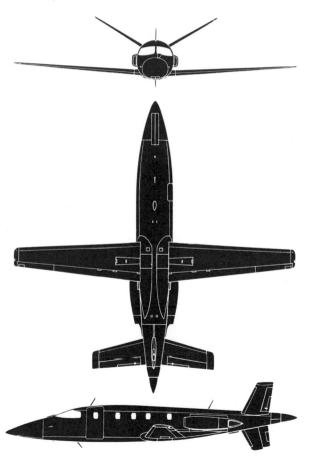

LOCKHEED L-100-30 HERCULES

Country of Origin: USA.

Type: Medium/long-range military and commercial freight transport.

Power Plant: Four 4,508 ehp Allison T56-A-15 turboprops.

Performance: Max cruise speed, 386 mph (620 km/h) at 20,000 ft (6 095 m); long-range cruise, 345 mph (556 km/h); range (max. payload), 2,300 mls (3 700 km); ferry range (with 2,265 Imp gal/10 296 l of external fuel), 5,354 mls (8 617 km).

Weights: Operational empty, 79,516 lb (36 068 kg); max take-off, 155,000 lb (70 310 kg).

Accommodation: Normal flight crew of four and provision for 97 casualty litters plus medical attendants, 128 combat troops or 92 paratroops. For pure freight role up to seven cargo pallets may be loaded.

Status: More than 1,700 Hercules (all versions) had been delivered by the beginning of 1984 when production was continuing at three monthly.

Notes: The L-100-30 and its military equivalent, the C-130H-30, are stretched versions of the basic Hercules, the C-130H. The original civil model, the L-100-20 featured a 100-in (2,54-m) fuselage stretch over the basic military model, and the L-100-30, intended for both military and civil application, embodies a further 80-in (2,03-m) stretch. Military operators of the C-130H-30 version are Algeria, Indonesia, Cameroun and Nigeria, and 30 of the RAF's Hercules C Mk 1s (equivalent of the C-130H) are being modified to C-130H-30 standards as Hercules C Mk 3s, most having been returned to service by the beginning of 1984 with the programme continuing into 1985.

LOCKHEED L-100-30 HERCULES

Dimensions: Span, 132 ft 7 in (40,41 m); length, 112 ft 9 in (34,37 m); height, 38 ft 3 in (11,66 m); wing area, 1,745 sq ft (162,12 m²).

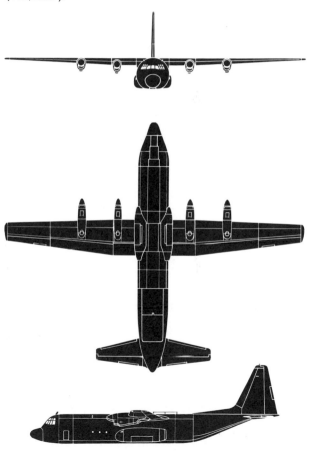

McDONNELL DOUGLAS AV-8B HARRIER II

Country of Origin: USA (and UK).

Type: Single-seat V/STOL ground attack aircraft.

Power Plant: One 21,180 lb st (9 607 kgp) Rolls-Royce F402-RR-406 Pegasus 11-21E (Mk 105) turbofan.

Performance: Max speed (clean aircraft) 668 mph (1 075 km/h) or Mach 0·88 at sea level, 614 mph (988 km/h) or Mach 0·93 at 36,000 ft (10 970 m); tactical radius (HI-LO-HI interdiction with seven 1,000-lb/453,6-kg bombs and 25-mm cannon), 692 mls (1 114 km); ferry range (with four 250 Imp/gal/1 136 l drop tanks), 2,876 mls (4 630 km).

Weights: Operational empty, 12,750 lb (5 783 kg); max take-off (for VTO), 19,185 lb (8 702 kg), (for STO), 29,750 lb (13 495 kg).

Armament: One 25-mm GAU-12/U five-barrel rotary cannon and up to 9,200 lb (4 173 kg) of ordnance on one fuselage centreline and six wing stations.

Status: First of four FSD (Full Scale Development) aircraft flown on 5 November 1981, with first of pilot batch of 12 aircraft for the US Marine Corps flown on 29 August 1983. The USMC has a requirement for 336 aircraft, and the RAF has an initial requirement for a further 60 (as Harrier GR Mk 5s), deliveries to the latter service being scheduled for 1986.

Notes: The AV-8B is a progressive development of the British Aerospace Harrier (see 1982 edition) currently serving with the RAF in GR Mk 3 and T Mk 4 forms, with USMC as the AV-8C and TAV-8A, and with the Spanish Navy as the Matador. The AV-8B Harrier II differs primarily in having a larger supercritical wing of composite construction, improved lift devices, extended rear fuselage and a raised cockpit. It has twice the payload or radius of action compared with the Harrier GR Mk 3.

McDONNELL DOUGLAS AV-8B HARRIER II

Dimensions: Span, 30 ft 4 in (9,24 m); length, 46 ft 4 in (14,12 m); height, 11 ft 8 in (3,55 m); wing area, 241 sq ft (22,40 m²).

McDONNELL DOUGLAS F-15C EAGLE

Country of Origin: USA.

Type: Single-seat air superiority fighter.

Power Plant: Two 14,780 lb st (6 705 kgp) dry and 23,904 lb st (10 855 kgp) reheat Pratt & Whitney F100-PW-100 turbofans.

Performance: Max speed (short-endurance dash), 1,676 mph (2 698 km/h) or Mach 2·54, (sustained), 1,518 mph (2 443 km/h) or Mach 2·3 at 40,000 ft (12 190 m); max endurance (internal fuel), 2·9 hrs, (with conformal pallets), 5·25 hrs; service ceiling, 63,000 ft (19 200 m).

Weights: Basic equipped, 28,700 lb (13 018 kg); loaded (full internal fuel and four AIM-7 AAMs), 44,500 lb (20 185 kg); max take-off, 68,000 lb (30 845 kg).

Armament: One 20-mm M-61A1 rotary cannon plus four AIM-7F Sparrow and four AIM-9L Sidewinder AAMs.

Status: First flown 26 February 1979, the F-15C is the second major single-seat production version of the Eagle, having, together with its two-seat equivalent, the F-15D, supplanted the F-15A and F-15B from the 444th aircraft mid 1980. The F-15C and D were the current production models at the beginning of 1984, with more than 800 (all versions) delivered, total USAF Eagle requirement being 969 aircraft.

Notes: Featuring upgraded avionics and conformal fuel packs, the F-15C is being supplied to Saudi Arabia (47 plus 15 F-15Ds) and 84 are being licence manufactured as F-15Js by Japan (including eight from knocked-down assemblies) which country is also receiving 12 F-15DJ two-seaters. Israel received 40 F-15 Eagles (since modified for conformal tanks) and is to receive a further 11 aircraft. The USAF has tested an all-weather interdiction F-15 retaining full air superiority capability. This carries air-to-ground weapons on the conformal tanks.

McDONNELL DOUGLAS F-15C EAGLE

Dimensions: Span, 42 ft 9¾ in (13,05 m); length, 63 ft 9 in (19,43 m); height, 18 ft 5½ in (5,63 m); wing area, 608 sq ft (56,50 m²).

McDONNELL DOUGLAS F-18A HORNET

Country of Origin: USA.

Type: Single-seat shipboard and shore-based multi-role fighter and attack aircraft.

Power Plant: Two 10,600 lb st (4810 kgp) dry and 15,800 lb st (7167 kgp) reheat General Electric F404-GE-400 turbofans.

Performance: Max speed (AAMs on wingtip and fuselage stations), 1,190 mph (1915 km/h) or Mach 1·8 at 40,000 ft (12150 m); initial climb (half fuel and wingtip AAMs), 60,000 ft/min (304,6 m/sec); tactical radius (combat air patrol on internal fuel), 480 mls (770 km), (with three 262 Imp gal/1192 l external tanks), 735 mls (1180 km).

Weights: Empty equipped, 28,000 lb (12700 kg); loaded (air superiority mission with half fuel and four AAMs), 35,800 lb (16240 kg); max take-off, 56,000 lb (25400 kg).

Armament: One 20-mm M-61A-1 rotary cannon and (air-air) two AIM-7E/F Sparrow and two AIM-9G/H Sidewinder AAMs, or (attack) up to 17,000 lb (7711 kg) of ordnance.

Status: First of 11 FSD (full-scale development) Hornets (including two TF-18A two-seaters) flown 18 November 1978. Planning at beginning of 1984 called for 1,366 Hornets for US Navy and US Marine Corps (including 153 TF-18As). First production F-18A flown April 1980.

Notes: Land-based versions of the Hornet have been ordered by Australia (57 F-18As and 18 TF-18As), Canada (113 CF-18As and 24 CF-18Bs) and Spain (84 F-18As and TF-18As). Separate F-18 fighter and A-18 attack versions of the Hornet were initially planned by the US Navy. Both roles were subsequently combined in a single basic version, and current planning calls for the inclusion of two Hornet squadrons in the complement of each of the large US Navy carriers.

McDONNELL DOUGLAS F-18A HORNET

Dimensions: Span, 37 ft 6 in (11,43 m); length, 56 ft 0 in (17,07 m); height, 15 ft 4 in (4,67 m); wing area, 396 sq ft (36,79 m²).

McDONNELL DOUGLAS KC-10A EXTENDER

Country of Origin: USA.

Type: Flight refuelling tanker and military freighter.

Power Plant: Three 52,500 lb st (23 814 kgp) General Electric CF6-50C2 turbofans.

Performance: Max speed, 620 mph (988 km/h) at 33,000 ft (10 060 m); max. cruise, 595 mph (957 km/h) at 31,000 ft (9 450 m); long-range cruise, 540 mph (870 km/h); typical refuelling mission, 2,200 mls (3 540 km) from base with 200,000 lb (90 720 kg) of fuel and return; max range (with 170,000 lb/77 112 kg freight), 4,370 mls (7 033 km).

Weights: Operational empty (tanker), 239,747 lb (108 749 kg), (cargo configuration), 243,973 lb (110 660 kg); max take-off, 590,000 lb (267 624 kg).

Accommodation: Flight crew of five plus provision for six seats for additional crew and four bunks for crew rest. Fourteen further seats may be provided for support personnel in the forward cabin. Alternatively, a larger area can be provided for 55 more support personnel, with necessary facilities, to increase total accommodation (including flight crew) to 80.

Status: First KC-10A was flown on 12 July 1980, with 16 ordered by the USAF by the beginning of 1983. A further 44 have been ordered under five-year contracting process for delivery through 1987. First operational KC-10A squadron was activated on 1 October 1981, and 20 had been delivered to the USAF by the beginning of 1984.

Notes: The KC-10A is a military tanker/freighter derivative of the commercial DC-10 Series 30 (see 1983 edition) with refuelling boom, boom operator's station, hose and drogue, military avionics and body fuel cells in the lower cargo compartments. The KC-10A is the first tanker developed from the outset to offer both flying-boom and probe-and-drogue refuelling.

McDONNELL DOUGLAS KC-10A EXTENDER

Dimensions: Span, 165 ft 4 in (50,42 m); length, 182 ft 0 in (55,47 m); height, 58 ft 1 in (17,70 m); wing area, 3,958 sq ft (367,7 m²).

McDONNELL DOUGLAS MD-80

Country of Origin: USA.
Type: Short/medium-haul commercial airliner.
Power Plant: Two 19,250 lb st (8730 kgp) Pratt & Whitney JT8D-209 turbofans.
Performance: Max cruising speed, 574 mph (924 km/h) at 27,000 ft (8230 m); econ cruise, 522 mph (840 km/h) at 33,000 ft (10060 m); long-range cruise, 505 mph 813 km/h) at 35,000 ft (10670 m); range (with max payload), 1,594 mls (2565 km) at econ cruise, (with max fuel), 3,280 mls (5280 km) at long-range cruise.
Weights: Operational empty, 77,797 lb (35289 kg); max take-off, 140,000 lb (63503 kg).
Accommodation: Flight crew of two and typical mixed-class arrangement for 23 first- and 137 economy-class passengers, or 155 all-economy or 172 commuter-type arrangements with five-abreast seating.
Status: First MD-80 flown (as Super 80) on 18 October 1979, with first customer delivery (to Swissair) on 12 September 1980, and 166 ordered by beginning of 1984 (excluding 35 aircraft being built for short-term lease) with 135 delivered by beginning of 1984, when production was four monthly.
Notes: The MD-80 is the largest of six members of the DC-9 family, the MD-82 sub-type having 20,850 lb st (9458 kgp) JT8D-217 engines with which it was certificated at a max take-off weight of 149,500 lb (67813 kg) in September 1982, this giving a max payload range of 2,300 mls (3700 km). Current development studies include the MD-83 with a max take-off weight of 160,000 lb (72576 kg) and a max payload range of the order of 2,880 mls (4630 km). Overall size will remain unchanged, but wings and undercarriage will be strengthened to cater for the additional fuel and increased weights. A total of 973 DC-9s (of which the MD-80 is a derivative type) was delivered, including 43 military C-9s.

McDONNELL DOUGLAS MD-80

Dimension: Span, 107 ft 10 in (32,85 m); length, 147 ft 10 in (45,08 m); height, 29 ft 4 in (8,93 m); wing area, 1,279 sq ft (118,8 m²).

MIKOYAN MIG-23 (FLOGGER)

Country of Origin: USSR.
Type: Single-seat (Flogger-B, E and G) air superiority and (Flogger-F and H) close air support fighter.
Power Plant: One 17,635 lb st (8 000 kgp) dry and 25,350 lb st (11 500 kgp) reheat Tumansky R-29B turbojet.
Performance: (Flogger-G) Max speed (clean aircraft with half fuel), 1,520 mph (2 446 km/h) or Mach 2·3 above 36,090 ft (11 000 m); combat radius (high-altitude air-air mission with four AAMs), 530 mls (850 km), (with centreline combat tank), 700 mls.
Weights: Normal loaded (clean), 34,170 lb (15 500 kg); max take-off, 44,312 lb (20 100 kg).
Armament: One 23-mm twin-barrel GSh-23L cannon and (B and G) two AA-7 Apex and two AA-8 Aphid, or (E) four AA-2-2 Advanced Atoll AAMs, or (F and H) up to 9,920 lb (4 500 kg) of bombs and missiles.
Status: Aerodynamic prototype of MiG-23 flown winter 1966-67, with service debut (Flogger-B) following 1971. Production rate of 50 (all versions) monthly continuing at beginning of 1984, when some 2,500 were estimated to be in Soviet service.
Notes: The Flogger-G (illustrated) is the latest air-air version of the MiG-23 in Soviet service, this being an improved variant of the Flogger-B (see 1982 edition) with revised vertical tail and other changes. Flogger-E is an export equivalent of Flogger-B, and Flogger-F and H are air-ground versions with redesigned forward fuselage essentially similar to that of the MiG-27 (see pages 148-9).

MIKOYAN MIG-23 (FLOGGER)

Dimensions: (Estimated) Span (17 deg sweep), 46 ft 9 in (14,25 m), (72 deg sweep), 27 ft 6 in (8,38 m); length (including probe), 55 ft 1½ in (16,80 m); wing area, 293·4 sq ft (27,26 m²).

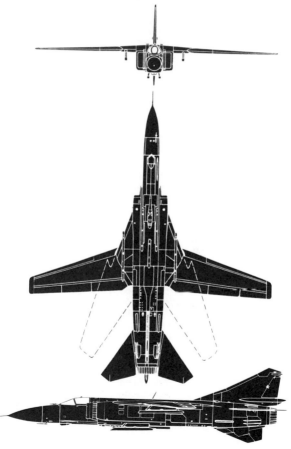

MIKOYAN MIG-25 (FOXBAT)

Country of Origin: USSR.
Type: Single-seat (Foxbat-A and -E) interceptor fighter and (Foxbat-B and -D) high-altitude reconnaissance aircraft.
Power Plant: Two 20,500 lb st (9 300 kgp) dry and 27,120 lb st (12 300 kgp) reheat Tumansky R-15 turbojets.
Performance: (Foxbat-A) Max speed (short-period dash with four AAMs), 1,850 mph (2 980 km/h) or Mach 2·8 above 36,000 ft (10 970 m); max speed at sea level, 650 mph (1 045 km/h) or Mach 0·85; initial climb, 40,950 ft/min (208 m/sec); service ceiling, 80,000 ft (24 385 m); combat radius (including allowance for Mach 2·5 intercept, 250 mls (400 km), (range optimised profile), 400 mls (645 km).
Weights: (Foxbat-A) Empty equipped, 44,100 lb (20 000 kg); max take-off, 77,160 lb (35 000 kg).
Armament: Four AA-6 Acrid AAMs (two semi-active radar homing and two IR-homing).
Status: The MiG-25 entered service (in Foxbat-A form) in 1970, the photo/ELINT recce version (Foxbat-B) following in 1971 and the optimised ELINT version (Foxbat-D) in 1974. Foxbat-As are being converted to Foxbat-E standard.
Notes: The Foxbat-A and Foxbat-C two-seat conversion trainer have been exported to Algeria, Libya and Syria, and the latter, together with Foxbat-B, to India. Foxbat-E (illustrated above) possesses limited look-down/shoot-down capability and uprated engines similar to those of Foxhound.

MIKOYAN MIG-25 (FOXBAT)

Dimensions: Span, 45 ft 9 in (13,94 m); length, 73 ft 2 in (22,30 m); height, 18 ft 4½ in (5,60 m); wing area, 602·8 sq ft (56,00 m²).

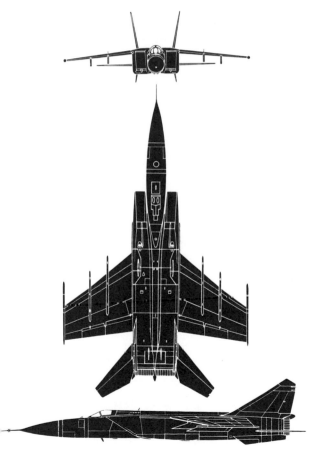

MIKOYAN MIG-27 (FLOGGER)

Country of Origin: USSR.

Type: Single-seat tactical strike and close air support fighter.

Power Plant: One 14,330 lb st (6 500 kgp) dry and 17,920 lb st (8 130 kgp) reheat Tumansky R-29-300 turbojet.

Performance: Max speed (clean aircraft with half fuel), 685 mph (1 102 km/h) or Mach 0·95 at 1,000 ft (305 m), 1,056 mph (1 700 km/h) or Mach 1·6 at 36,090 ft (11 000 m); combat radius (HI-LO-HI mission profile on internal fuel with 4,410 lb/2 000 kg external ordnance), 310 mls (500 km).

Weights: (Estimated) Normal loaded (clean), 35,000 lb (15 875 kg); max take-off, 45,000 lb (20 410 kg).

Armament: One 23-mm six-barrel rotary cannon and up to 7,716 lb (3 500 kg) of external ordnance on five stations.

Status: Evolved from the MiG-23 (see pages 144-5) as a dedicated air-ground aircraft, the MiG-27 is believed to have first entered service (in Flogger-D) form in 1975-76, with production continuing (in Flogger-J form) at the beginning of 1984. Licence production is to be undertaken in India with deliveries commencing in 1986.

Notes: Whereas the Flogger-F and H are minimum-change air-ground derivatives of the MiG-23, the MiG-27 has been tailored closely for ground attack. The forward fuselage is similar to that of the Flogger-F and H, apart from augmented side armour, but the rough-field undercarriage has necessitated bulging of the fuselage and a modified turbofan is installed with larger-area fixed intakes and shorter afterburner nozzle. The Flogger-J (illustrated) has a lengthened nose and wing leading-edge extensions.

148

MIKOYAN MIG-27 (FLOGGER)

Dimensions: (Estimated) Span (17 deg sweep), 46 ft 9 in (14,25 m), (72 deg sweep), 27 ft 6 in (8,38 m); length, 54 ft 0 in (16,46 m); wing area, 293·4 sq ft (27,26 m²).

MIKOYAN MIG-29 (FULCRUM)

Country of Origin: USSR.
Type: Single-seat air superiority fighter.
Power Plant: Two 13,000 lb st (5 897 kgp) dry and 19,000 lb st (8 620 kgp) re-heat turbofans.
Performance: (Estimated) Max speed, 1,518 mph (2 445 km/h) above 36,100 ft (11 000 m), or Mach 2·3, 915 mph (1 470 km/h) at sea level, or Mach 1·2; initial climb, 50,000 ft/min (254 m/sec); radius (clean), 440 mls (710 km), (with four AAMs), 415 mls (670 km), (with four 1,100-lb/500-kg bombs), 375 mls (600 km).
Weights: (Estimated) Empty, 28,000 lb (12 700 kg); loaded, 36,000 lb (16 330 kg).
Armament: One 30-mm cannon and up to eight air-to-air missiles.
Status: The MiG-29 was first seen at Ramenskoye in the spring of 1979, at which time it was referred to as the Ram-L for identification purposes. Production was presumably initiated in 1981, and initial operational capability is anticipated in 1984.
Notes: The MiG-29 is believed to be in the general category of the F-16 and to be nearer to initial deployment than the Sukhoi Su-27 (see pages 206–7). Like the MiG-31 and Su-27, the MiG-29 possesses lookdown/shootdown radar capability, infra red search and track, and digital data link, and will presumably supplant the MiG-21 in the air superiority role.

MIKOYAN MIG-29 (FULCRUM)

Dimensions: (Estimated) Span, 34 ft 5 in (10,50 m); length, 50 ft 10 in (15,50 m); wing area, 380 sq ft (35,30 m²).

MIKOYAN MIG-31 (FOXHOUND)

Country of Origin: USSR.
Type: Tandem two-seat interceptor fighter.
Power Plant: Two 30,865 lb st (14 000 kgp) reheat Tumansky R-15-300 turbojets.
Performance: (Estimated) Max speed, 1,520 mph (2 445 km/h) above 36,100 ft (11 000 m), or Mach 2·3, 915 mph (1 472 km/h) at sea level; max operational radius (with external fuel),1,180 mls (1 900 km); ceiling, 80 000 ft (24 385 m).
Weights: (Estimated) Empty equipped, 45,000 lb (20 410 kg); normal loaded, 65,200 lb (29 575 kg).
Armament: Up to eight AA-9 radar-guided air-to-air missiles.
Status: The MiG-31 has been under development since the mid 'seventies and is believed to have been first deployed in 1982, with some four regiments equipped with this type by the beginning of 1984.
Notes: The MiG-31 has been derived from the MiG-25 (see 146–147) and features a redesigned forward fuselage housing a lookdown-shootdown pulse Doppler weapons system and tandem cockpits for the pilot and systems operator. Some indication of the capability of the MiG-31 came in 1978, when a Soviet official announcement indicated that, during tests, presumably a prototype flying at around 6 000 m (19 685 ft) had detected a target flying below 60 m (200 ft) at a range of 20 km (12·5 mls), fired an unarmed missile against it and achieved a theoretical kill. The Tumansky engines installed in the MiG-31 are fundamentally similar to those employed by the MiG-25 derivative, referred to as the Ye-266M, which established a series of world height records.

MIKOYAN MIG-31 (FOXHOUND)

Dimensions: (Estimated) Span, 45 ft 9 in (13,94 m); length, 68 ft 10 in (21,00 m); height, 18 ft 6 in (5,63 m); wing area, 602·8 sq ft (56,00 m²).

MITSUBISHI MU-300 DIAMOND IA

Country of Origin: Japan.
Type: Light corporate transport.
Power Plant: Two 2,625 lb st (1 190 kgp) Pratt & Whitney (Canada) JT15D-4D turbofans.
Performance: Max speed (at 12,000 lb/5 443 kg), 501 mph (806 km/h) at 30,000 ft (9 150 m); typical cruise, 466 mph (750 km/h) at 39,000 ft (11 890 m); range cruise, 432 mph (695 km/h); max range (with four passengers and VFR reserves), 1,765 mls (2 840 km).
Weights: Empty equipped, 9,100 lb (4 128 kg); max take-off, 16,230 lb (7 362 kg).
Accommodation: Pilot and co-pilot/passenger on flight deck and various arrangements for up to nine passengers in main cabin.
Status: First of two prototypes of Diamond I flown on 29 August 1978, with first production aircraft following on 21 May 1981. US certification acquired 6 November 1981. Customer deliveries of Diamond IA were scheduled to commence in January 1984, and a higher-performance version, the Diamond II, was announced in October 1983.
Notes: The Diamond IA differs from the original production Diamond I in having uprated (5 per cent) engines with thrust reversers and a series of refinements improving balanced field length and cruise performance. The Diamond II will have the same airframe as the Diamond IA, but will be powered by 2,900 lb st (1 315 kgp) JT15D-5 turbofans which will result in a max cruise of 525 mph (844 km/h) at 13,000 lb (5 897 kg) and a 1,820-mile (2 926-km) range with six passengers and VFR reserves. An optional long-range tank will be available.

MITSUBISHI MU-300 DIAMOND IA

Dimensions: Span, 43 ft 5 in (13,23 m); length, 48 ft 4 in (14,73 m); height, 13 ft 9 in (4,19 m); wing area, 241·4 sq ft (22,43 m²).

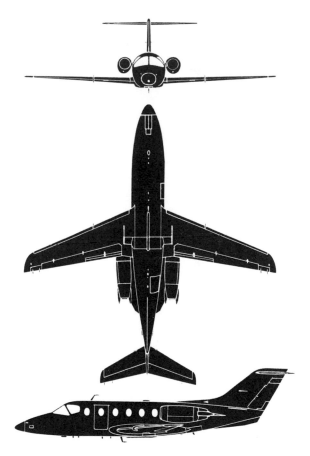

MOONEY 301

Country of Origin: USA.
Type: Light cabin monoplane.
Power Plant: One 360 hp Avco Lycoming TIO-540-R six-cylinder horizontally-opposed engine.
Performance: Max speed (at 3,800 lb/1 724 kg), 301 mph (484 km/km/h); max cruise, 259 mph (417 km/h); initial climb, 1,450 ft/min (18,29 m/sec); range (at 75% power with reserves), 1,150 mls (1 850 km) at 25,000 ft (7 620 m).
Weights: Empty, 2,548 lb (1 156 kg); max take-off, 4,000 lb (1 814 kg).
Accommodation: Pilot and co-pilot/passenger side-by-side and standard club arrangement in main cabin fof four passengers.
Status: Prototype flown in April 1983, with certification and initial customer deliveries planned for the second half of 1986.
Notes: The pressurised Mooney 301 possesses no commonality with the unpressurised Models 201 and 231 currently manufactured by this company, being an entirely new design. It has a new advanced laminar-flow wing of Eppler section, Fowler flaps extending over some 80 per cent of the wing trailing edge and upper wing surface spoilers for roll control aided by small ailerons at the wingtips. Pressurization provides a cabin altitude equivalent to 8,000 ft (2 440 m) at the anticipated certificated altitude of 25,000 ft (7 620 m). The eventual development of a turboprop-powered version of the Mooney 301 is foreseen.

MOONEY 301

Dimensions: Span, 36 ft 9 in (11,20 m); length, 29 ft 9¼ in (9,07 m); height, 9 ft 10¾ in (3,02 m); wing area, 150 sq ft (13,93 m²).

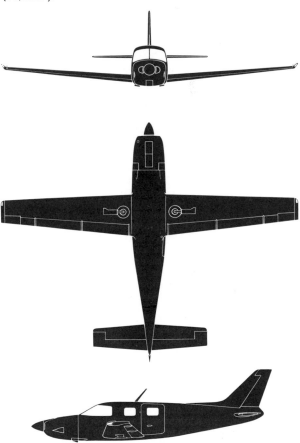

MOONEY TX-1

Country of Origin: USA.

Type: Side-by-side two-seat primary/basic trainer.

Power Plant: One 240 hp Continental TSIO-360-GB six-cylinder horizontally-opposed engine.

Performance: Max speed, 207 mph (333 km/h) at sea level, 240 mph (386 km/h) at 16,000 ft (4 875 m); cruise (75% power), 185 mph (298 km/h) at sea level, 212 mph (341 km/h) at 16,000 ft (4 875 m), 231 mph (372 km/h) at 25,000 ft (7 620 m); initial climb, 1,336 ft/min (6,79 m/sec); range (no reserves at sea level), 734 mls (1 181 km) at 75% power, 830 mls (1 336 km) at 65% power, 940 mls (1 513 km) at 55% power; max endurance, 11·3 hrs at 144 mph (232 km/h) at 8,000 ft (2 440 m).

Weights: Empty, 1,800 lb (816 kg); max take-off, 2,900 lb (1 315 kg).

Armament: Gun pods, ASMs or practice bombs on four wing pylons.

Status: The prototype TX-1 (MT-20) entered flight test late 1982. No decision regarding series production had been taken by the end of 1983.

Notes: The TX-1 is derived from Mooney's M20 series of four-seat high-performance cabin monoplanes, the current production versions of which are the M20J (Model 201) and M20K (Model 231), the latter having a turbo-supercharged engine. The TX-1 is based on the M20K from which it differs primarily in respect of the cockpit which is enclosed by a one-piece aft-sliding canopy, and is intended to fulfil several military roles, including aerobatic training (stressed for +6*g* to −4*g*), weapon delivery training and limited tactical strike carrying internal wing radar. It is also suitable for observation, liaison and forward air control missions with camera pods, surveillance equipment, etc, as necessary.

MOONEY TX-1

Dimensions: Span, 36 ft 1 in (10,99 m); length, 25 ft 5 in (7,75 m); height, 8 ft 4 in (2,54 m); wing area, 174·79 sq ft (16,24 m²).

NDN-IT TURBO FIRECRACKER

Country of Origin: United Kingdom.
Type: Tandem two-seat basic/advanced trainer.
Power Plant: One 550 shp Pratt & Whitney (Canada) PT6A-25A turboprop.
Performance: Max speed, 261 mph (421 km/h) at 15,000 ft (4 570 m); initial climb (at 3,400 lb/1 542 kg), 2,390 ft/min (12,14 m/sec); range (internal fuel with no reserves), 576 mls (927 km/h) at 10,000 ft (3 050 m).
Weights: Empty equipped, 2,350 lb (1 066 kg); normal max (without overload), 3,400 lb (1 542 kg).
Armament: Four wing hardpoints for various ordnance loads for both training and light strike tasks.
Status: First NDN-IT flown on 1 September 1983, and this, together with two additional aircraft, being supplied to Specialist Flying Training Ltd.
Notes: Derived from the piston-engined NDN-1 Firecracker, the NDN-1T has been developed primarily to meet the requirements of the RAF for a Jet Provost replacement over the 1986-89 timeframe. The Turbo Firecracker features a unique low aspect ratio wing which reproduces the roll yaw characteristics and low-speed sink rates of pure jet swept- and delta-wing combat aircraft. It is also unique among contemporary turboprop-powered trainers in featuring a speed brake. It is capable of accepting the 750 shp PT6A-25C engine and has Centrisep (Centrifugal Separator) particle separator screens over its lateral air intakes. Provision is made for installation of a Stencel Ranger rocket-assisted cockpit escape system possessing zero-zero capability. Firecracker Aircraft can produce one-two monthly in its existing facilities, but a large series order will necessitate selection of an industrial partner.

NDN-1T TURBO FIRECRACKER

Dimensions: Span, 26 ft 0 in (7,92 m); length, 27 ft 4 in (8,33 m); height, 10 ft 8 in (3,25 m); wing area, 128 sq ft (11,89 m²).

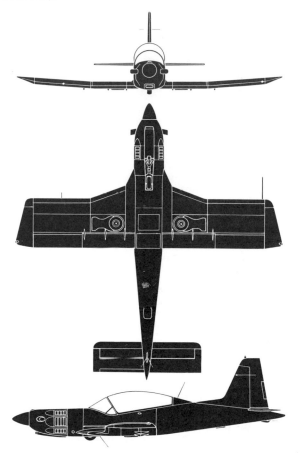

NORTHROP F-20A TIGERSHARK

Country of Origin: USA.

Type: Single-seat multi-role fighter.

Power Plant: One 17,000 lb st (7 711 kgp) reheat General Electric F404-GE-F1G1 turbofan.

Performance: Max speed, 1,320 mph (2 124 km/h) or Mach 2·0 above 36,000 ft (10 975 m), 800 mph (1 288 km/h) or Mach 1·05 at sea level; initial climb at combat weight (50% internal fuel and wingtip missiles), 52,800 ft/min (268,2 m/sec); combat ceiling, 54,700 ft (16 672 m); time to 40,000 ft (12 190 m) from brakes release, 2·3 min; tactical radius with two 229 Imp gal/1 040 l drop tanks and 20 min reserve at sea level (HI-LO-HI interdiction with seven Mk 82 bombs), 437 mls (704 km), (combat air patrol with 96 min on station), 345 mls (555 km); ferry range (max fuel), 1,842 mls (2 965 km).

Weights: Take-off (clean), 18,005 lb (8 167 kg); max take-off, 26,290 lb (11 925 kg).

Armament: Two 20-mm M-39 cannon and up to 7,000 lb (3 175 kg) of external ordnance on five stations.

Status: Two Tigersharks flown on 30 August 1982 and 26 August 1983 respectively. Deliveries offered 18-24 months of receipt of order.

Notes: The Tigershark is an advanced derivative of the F-5E Tiger II (see 1981 edition) with a low-bypass turbofan affording 70 per cent more thrust than the twin engines of the earlier fighter, integrated digital avionics, including a digital flight control system, and a multi-mode coherent pulse-Doppler radar. The second prototype (illustrated) features a new cockpit canopy offering 45 per cent more transparency area. On 1 December 1983, this prototype flew unrefuelled across the USA, covering the 2,308 miles (3 714 km) in 3 hrs 47 min.

NORTHROP F-20A TIGERSHARK

Dimensions: Span, 26 ft 8 in (8,13 m); length, 46 ft 6 in (14,17 m); height, 13 ft 10 in (4,22 m); wing area, 186 sq ft (17,28 m²).

OMAC I

Country of Origin: USA.

Type: Light corporate executive transport.

Power Plant: One 700 shp Avco Lycoming LTP 101-700A-1A turboprop.

Performance: Max speed, 322 mph (519 km/h); high-speed cruise, 299 mph (482 km/h); econ cruise, 250 mph (402 km/h); initial climb, 2,000 ft/min (10,2 m/sec); ceiling, 25,000 ft (7 620 m); max range (with 60 min reserves), 3,137 mls (5 050 km).

Weights: Empty, 3,500 lb (1 587 kg); max take-off, 6,500 lb (2 948 kg).

Accommodation: Pilot and co-pilot/passenger side-by-side plus four-six passengers in main cabin.

Status: First of two prototypes flown on 11 December 1981, with second following on 19 February 1983, and certification planned for December 1984. Firm orders had been placed for some 40 aircraft by the beginning of 1984.

Notes: Expected to achieve production status in 1985, after a somewhat protracted development during which numerous modifications have been incorporated, the OMAC I is, like the Beechcraft Starship (see pages 32–33), of canard, or tail-first, arrangement. Since initial testing, the first prototype (illustrated) has been fitted with a completely new fuselage and a redesigned foreplane, and the angles of the wingtip vertical surfaces have been changed several times. It is anticipated that OMAC Incorporated will manufacture the wings and fuselages of production aircraft, all other components and assemblies being manufactured by other companies under sub-contract. OMAC will retain responsibility for final assembly and flight testing.

OMAC I

Dimensions: Span, 38 ft 4⅔ in (11,70 m); length, 29 ft 5⅞ in (8,99 m); height, 11 ft 5¾ in (3,50 m); wing area (including foreplane), 319·7 sq ft (29,70 m²).

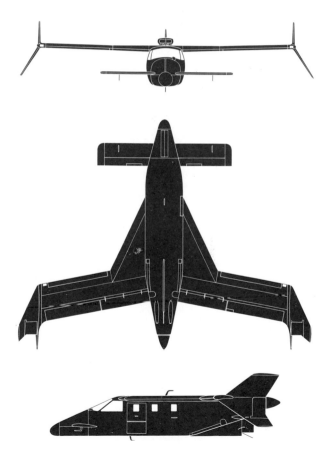

PANAVIA TORNADO F MK 2

Country of Origin: United Kingdom.
Type: Tandem two-seat interceptor fighter.
Power Plant: Two (approx) 9,000 lb st (4 082 kgp) dry and 16,000 lb st (7 258 kgp) reheat Turbo-Union RB.199-34R-04 Mk 101 (Improved) turbofans.
Performance: (Estimated) Max speed, 920 mph (1 480 km/h) or Mach 1·2 at sea level, 1,450 mph (2 333 km/h) or Mach 2·2 at 40,000 ft (12 190 m); radius of action (combat air patrol with two 330 Imp gal/1 500 l drop tanks and allowance for two hours loiter), 350–450 mls (560–725 km); time to 30,000 ft (9 145 m) from brakes release, 1·7 min; ferry range, 2,650 mls (4 265 km).
Weights: (Estimated) Empty equipped, 25,000 lb (11 340 kg); max take-off, 52,000 lb (23 587 kg).
Armament: One 27-mm IWKA-Mauser cannon, plus two AIM-9L Sidewinder and four BAe Sky Flash AAMs.
Status: First of three Tornado F Mk 2 prototypes flown on 27 October 1979, with production deliveries of 165–185 for the RAF commencing early 1984 and initial operational capability late 1984–early 1985.
Notes: The F Mk 2 is a UK-only derivative of the multi-national (UK, Federal Germany and Italy) multi-role fighter (see 1978 edition) which entered operational service with the RAF and the Federal German *Luftwaffe* and *Marineflieger* during 1982. Retaining 80 per cent commonality with the multi-role version, the F Mk 2 features a redesigned nose for the intercept radar and a lengthened fuselage which increases internal fuel capacity and permits the mounting of four Sky Flash missiles on fuselage stations. Emphasis is placed on range and endurance in order to mount combat air patrols at considerable distances from the British coastline, and the aircraft is fitted with a permanently-installed retractable air-refuelling probe.

PANAVIA TORNADO F MK 2

Dimensions: Span (25 deg sweep), 45 ft 7¼ in (13,90 m), (68 deg sweep), 28 ft 2½ in (8,59 m); length, 59 ft 3 in (18,06 m); height, 18 ft 8½ in (5,70 m); wing area, 322·9 sq ft (30,00 m²).

PARTENAVIA AP68TP/300 SPARTACUS

Country of Origin: Italy.
Type: Light multi-role transport and utility aircraft.
Power Plant: Two 330 shp Allison 250-B17C turboprops.
Performance: Max cruising speed, 240 mph (386 km/h) at 15,000 ft (4 570 m); range cruise, 190 mph (306 km/h) at 12,000 ft (3 660 m); initial climb, 2,057 ft/min (10,45 m/sec); service ceiling, 25,000 ft (7 620 m); range (with 1,600-lb/726-kg payload), 378 mls (609 km) at max cruise at 12,000 ft (3 660 m), (with 820-lb/327-kg payload), 1,237 mls (1 991 km) at 207 mph (333 km/h) at 20,000 ft (6 095 m).
Weights: Empty, 3,241 lb (1 470 kg); operational empty, 3,307 lb (1 500 kg); max take-off, 5,732 lb (2 600 kg).
Accommodation: Pilot and co-pilot/passenger in cockpit with three rows of paired individual seats in main cabin, the rearmost row being replaceable by a bench-type seat for three.
Status: The AP68TP/300, first flown on 29 March 1983, is the production derivative of the AP68TP/100 which entered flight test on 20 November 1981, and was, itself, derived from the AP68TP which made its initial flight on 11 September 1978. Initial customer deliveries are scheduled for the summer of 1984.
Notes: The Spartacus is a turboprop-powered derivative of the P68 series of piston-engined light twins and is a multi-role aircraft with both civil and military applications. The series /300 differs from the pre-series /100 primarily in having a conventional horizontal tail in place of an all-flying tailplane. A pressurised version is seen as a long-term objective.

PARTENAVIA AP68TP300 SPARTACUS

Dimensions: Span, 39 ft 4½ in (12,00 m); length, 31 ft 9¾ in (9,70 m); height, 12 ft 0 in (3,65 m); wing area, 200·22 sq ft (18,60 m²).

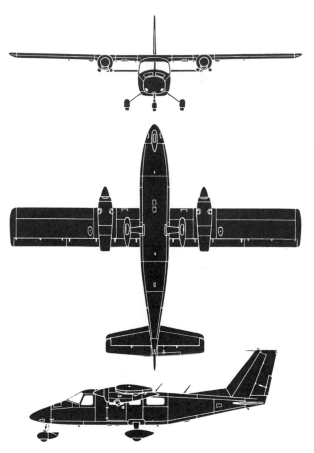

PILATUS PC-7 TURBO TRAINER

Country of Origin: Switzerland.
Type: Tandem two-seat basic trainer.
Power Plant: One 550 shp Pratt & Whitney (Canada) PT6A-25A turboprop.
Performance: Max continuous speed, 255 mph (411 km/h) at 10,000 ft (3 050 m); econ cruise, 230 mph (370 km/h) at 20,000 ft (6 100 m); initial climb, 2,065 ft/min (10,4 m/sec); service ceiling, 31,000 ft (9 450 m); max range (internal fuel), 650 mls (1 047 km).
Weights: Empty equipped, 2,932 lb (1 330 kg); max aerobatic, 4,188 lb (1 900 kg); max take-off, 5,952 lb (2 700 kg).
Armament: (Training or light strike) Six wing hardpoints permit external loads up to max of 2,292 lb (1 040 kg).
Status: First of two PC-7 prototypes flown 12 April 1966, and first production example flown 18 August 1978, with first customer deliveries (to Burma) following early 1979. The 200th PC-7 was rolled out on 30 July 1982, and total sales exceeded 340 aircraft by the beginning of 1984, with some 300 aircraft delivered and production continuing at a rate of six monthly.
Notes: The PC-7 is a derivative of the piston-engined P-3, and has been selected by 12 air forces and naval air arms as follows: Angola (12), Abu Dhabi (14), Austria (6), Bolivia (36), Burma (17), Chile (10), Guatemala (12), Iran, Iraq (52), Malaysia (44), Mexico (55) and Switzerland (40). The PC-7 has also been adopted by the Swissair airline pilot training school and the Centre de Formation Aéronautique in France. The example illustrated above is the first PC-7 to be sold to a US customer, delivery having been effected in May 1983. Follow-on buys were being discussed at the beginning of 1984 with several of the previously listed customers.

PILATUS PC-7 TURBO TRAINER

Dimensions: Span, 34 ft 1½ in (10,40 m); length, 31 ft 11⅞ in (9,75 m); height, 10 ft 6⅓ in (3,21 m); wing area, 178·68 sq ft (16,60 m²).

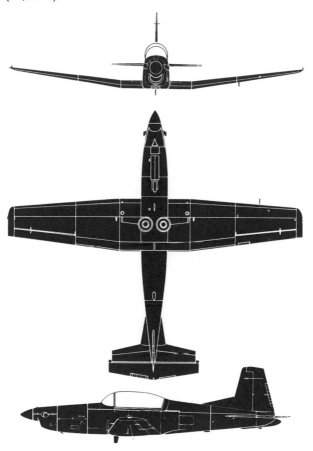

PIPER PA-42 CHEYENNE IV

Country of Origin: USA.

Type: Light corporate executive transport.

Power Plant: Two 1,000 shp Garrett TPE331-14 turboprops.

Performance: (Estimated) Max cruising speed, 404 mph (650 km/h) at 22,500 ft (6 860 m); initial climb, 3,400 ft/min (17,27 m/sec); time to 35,000 ft (10 670 m), 14 min; service ceiling, 41,000 ft (12 495 m); range (eight passengers and IFR reserves), 1,360 mls (2 187 km); max range (with 45 min reserves), 2,590 mls (4 170 km).

Weights: Empty, 7,050 lb (3 198 kg); max take-off, 11,950 lb (5 420 kg).

Accommodation: Flight crew of one or two on separate flight deck and various optional arrangements for six to nine passengers in main cabin.

Status: First of three prototypes of the Cheyenne IV commenced flight test 23 February 1983, with certification following March 1984 and initial customer deliveries in May of that year.

Notes: The Cheyenne IV is a re-engined derivative of the Cheyenne III (see 1982 edition) which is powered by 720 shp PT6A-41 turboprops. The airframe of the Cheyenne IV is basically similar to that of the III and is externally little changed, but the fuselage structure has been strengthened to cater for a 10,000 ft (3 050 m) cabin pressure up to 41,000 ft (12 495 m) and the larger-diameter four-bladed Dowty Rotol composite propellers that replace the three-bladed Hartzell Q-tip propellers have necessitated adoption of a lengthened undercarriage. The engine nacelle extension baggage compartments of the Cheyenne III have been eliminated and the nose baggage compartment has been enlarged.

PIPER PA-42 CHEYENNE IV

Dimensions: Span, 47 ft 8⅛ in (14,53 m); length, 43 ft 4¾ in (13,23 m); height, 15 ft 6 in (4,72 m); wing area, 293 sq ft (27,20 m²).

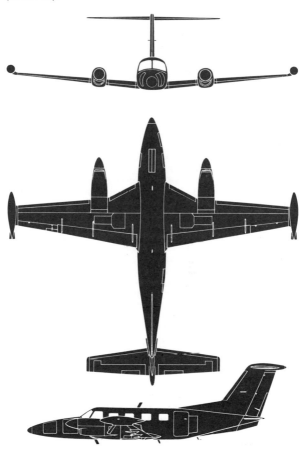

PIPER PA-46-310P MALIBU

Country of Origin: USA.
Type: Light cabin monoplane.
Power Plant: One 310 hp Continental TSIO-520-BE six-cylinder horizontally-opposed engine.
Performance: Max speed, 254 mph (409 km/h) at optimum altitude; cruise (75% power), 239 mph (385 km/h), 65% power), 225 mph (363 km/h); initial climb, 1,143 ft/min (5,8 m/sec); range (with 45 min reserves), 1,542 mls (2 482 km) at 75% power, 1,657 mls (2 667 km) at 65% power, 1,830 mls (2 945 km) at 55% power.
Weights: Standard empty, 2,275 lb (1 032 kg); max take-off, 3,850 lb (1 746 kg).
Accommodation: Pilot and five passengers in paired individual seats with rear airstair door.
Status: First prototype Malibu flown late 1980, with production prototype aircraft flying August 1982. Certification was obtained autumn 1983, with first delivery to a dealer following.
Notes: Intended to compete with the Cessna P210 Centurion, which, prior to the advent of the Malibu, was the sole pressurised single-engined cabin monoplane on the market, this new Piper aircraft is claimed to be the first production single-engined general aviation model to utilise computer-aided design and manufacturing (CAD/CAM) techniques. Possessing no relationship to previous Piper designs, the Malibu offers a cabin of "business twin" proportions with club seating and a rear airstair door, and is designed to give an 8,000 ft (2 440 m) cabin pressure up to 25,000 ft (7 620 m), at which the intercooling techniques of the TSIO-520 engine result in 240 hp still being available.

PIPER PA-46-310P MALIBU

Dimensions: Span, 43 ft 0 in (13,10 m); length, 28 ft 4¾ in (8,66 m); height, 11 ft 3½ in (3,44 m); wing area, 175 sq ft (16,26 m²).

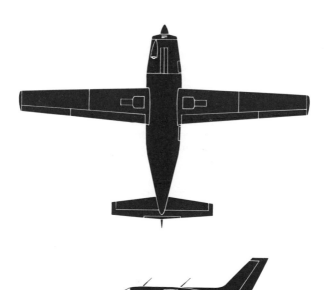

PIPER PA-48 ENFORCER

Country of Origin: USA.
Type: Single-seat close air support aircraft.
Power Plant: One 2,445 shp Avco Lycoming T55-L-9A turbo-prop.
Performance: Max speed, 363 mph (584 km/h); cruise, 254 mph (408 km/h) at 15,000 ft (4 575 m); initial climb, 2,500 ft/min (12,7 m/sec); service ceiling, 20,000 ft (6 100 m); combat radius (with two GPU-5/A 30-mm gun pods), 460 mls (740 km).
Weights: Empty, 7,200 lb (3 266 kg); operational equipped, 7,885 lb (3 576 kg); max take-off, 14,000 lb (6 350 kg).
Armament: Five hardpoints in each wing capable of lifting total external ordnance load of 5,680 lb (2 576 kg), with up to 2,000 lb (907 kg) on innermost hardpoint on each side.
Status: First and second prototypes flown on 9 April and 8 July 1983 respectively, with flight test programme continuing at beginning of 1984.
Notes: The PA-48 Enforcer is derived from the North American Mustang fighter of WWII, but possesses less than 10 per cent component part commonality with its precursor. Should the Enforcer be ordered into production it is foreseen that the present engine will be replaced by a 3,000 shp power plant. The Enforcer will be available in three versions—Close Air Support (CAS) I, II and III. CAS I will be the basic aircraft with fixed gunsight, internal 0·5-in (12,7-mm) guns and six wing hardpoints for a 4,500-lb (2 041-kg) bomb load; CAS II will have no internal guns and 10 wing hardpoints, and CAS III will have a headup display as standard and provision for six pylon tanks plus six ordnance hardpoints.

PIPER PA-48 ENFORCER

Dimensions: Span, 41 ft 4 in (12,60 m); length, 34 ft 2 in (10,41 m); height, 13 ft 1 in (3,99 m); wing area, 257 sq ft (23,87 m²).

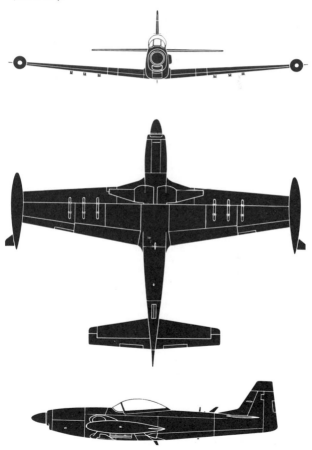

REIMS-CESSNA F-406 CARAVAN II

Countries of Origin: France and USA.
Type: Corporate and light utility transport.
Power Plant: Two 500 shp Pratt & Whitney PT6A-112 turbo-props.
Performance: Max cruising speed, 284 mph (458 km/h) at 15,000 ft (4 570 m); initial climb, 1,835 ft/min (9,3 m/sec); service ceiling, 31,000 ft (9 450 m); range at max cruise (with allowances and 45 min reserves), 1,476 mls (2 375 km) at 10,000 ft (3 050 m).
Weights: Standard empty, 4,788 lb (2 172 kg); max take-off, 9,299 lb (4 218 kg).
Accommodation: Pilot and co-pilot on flight deck and up to 12 passengers in main cabin.
Status: Prototype flown on 22 September 1983, with certification scheduled for the summer of 1984 and initial customer deliveries commencing during third quarter of year.
Notes: The Caravan II is a collaborative venture between Reims Aviation of France and Cessna Aircraft Company of the USA, which, relying quite heavily upon several exclusively Cessna twin-engined aircraft for many of its components, is assembled solely in France. Cessna manufactures all Caravan II components and assemblies that are common to other US-built aircraft, the fuselage being essentially that of the Titan, but incorporating the Conquest I nose and the Conquest II empennage, and the wings are those of the Conquest II with redesigned nacelles to accommodate the PT6A engines. Reims is responsible for French and US certification. There is no commonality between the Caravan II and the Caravan I (described and illustrated on pages 66-67).

178

REIMS-CESSNA F-406 CARAVAN II

Dimensions: Span, 49 ft 6 in (15,09 m); length, 39 ft 0$\frac{1}{4}$ in (11,89 m); height, 13 ft 1$\frac{1}{2}$ in (4,01 m); wing area, 252·74 sq ft.

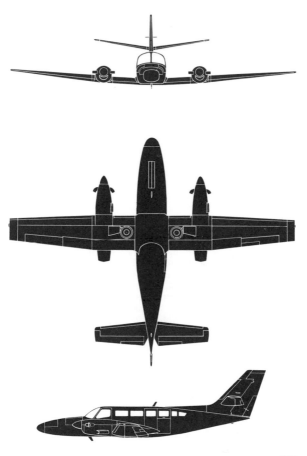

RHEIN-FLUGZEUGBAU FANTRAINER

Country of Origin: Federal Germany.
Type: Tandem two-seat primary/basic trainer.
Power Plant: One (Fantrainer 400) 420 shp Allison 250-C20B or (Fantrainer 600) 600 shp Allison 250-C30 turboshaft driving a five-bladed ducted fan.
Performance: (Fantrainer 400) Max speed, 230 mph (370 km/h) at 10,000 ft (3 050 m); initial climb, 2,000 ft/min (10,2 m/sec); range (no reserves), 1,094 mls (1 760 km). (Fantrainer 600) Max speed, 267 mph (430 km/h) at 18,000 ft (5 485 m); cruise, 230 mph (370 km/h) at 10,000 ft (3 050 m); initial climb, 3,150 ft/min (16 m/sec); range (no reserves), 846 mls (1 390 km/h).
Weights: (Fantrainer 400) Empty, 2,070 lb (939 kg); max take-off, 3,484 lb (1 580 kg). (Fantrainer 600) Empty, 2,340 lb (1 060 kg); max take-off, 5,070 lb (2 300 kg).
Status: First of two prototypes flown 27 October 1977, and first production aircraft (Fantrainer 600) having been scheduled to fly in January 1984, this being the first of four aircraft for delivery in flyaway condition to Thailand which has ordered 47 (31 Fantrainer 400s and 16 Fantrainer 600s) for delivery in kit form and has taken an option on 16 more (Fantrainer 600s). Fantrainers assembled in Thailand are to be fitted with wings of Thai manufacture and will be completed at a rate of two monthly increasing to six monthly in 1985. The first two Fantrainer 400s were to be delivered in March 1984.
Notes: Claimed to minimise the problems of transition to an advanced jet trainer by offering pure jet flight characteristics, the Fantrainer is of unconventional design. The production Fantrainer differs from the first prototype illustrated above in having a revised cockpit canopy (as illustrated opposite) and a Stencel Ranger rocket-assisted escape system.

RHEIN-FLUGSEUGBAU FANTRAINER

Dimensions: Span, 31 ft 10 in (9,70 m); length, 29 ft 6 in (9,00 m); height, 9 ft 6 in (2,90 m); wing area, 149·6 sq ft (13.90 m²).

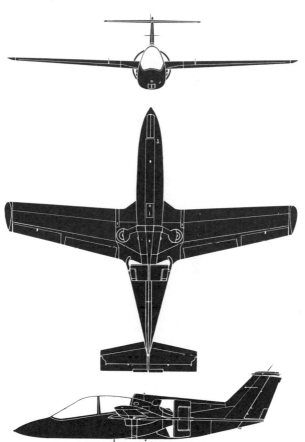

ROBIN ATL

Country of Origin: France.

Type: Side-by-side two-seat primary trainer and club aircraft.

Power Plant: On 47 hp JPX PAL 1300 three-cylinder two-stroke engine.

Performance: Max speed, 119 mph (180 km/h); econ cruise, 84·5 mph (136 km/h) at 7,000 ft (2 135 m) at 50% power; initial climb, 570 ft/min (2,90 m/sec); service ceiling, 13,500 ft (4 120 m); range, 497 mls (800 km); endurance, 5 hr 50 min.

Weights: Empty, 441 lb (200 kg); max take-off, 926 lb (420 kg).

Status: Prototype flown on 17 June 1983, with current planning calling for the production of 25 in 1984, 75 in 1985 and 100 annually thereafter.

Notes: The Robin ATL (*Avion Très Léger*) has been designed with the objective of achieving the lowest possible initial cost combined with the lowest possible operating cost in an attempt to arrest the upward spiral in the cost of flying and the impact of economic factors generally upon the flying movement. In order to make this venture practical, an entirely new engine has been developed specifically for the ATL. The ATL employs mixed construction, with Dacron-covered single-spar wooden wings with metal ailerons and electrically-operated plain flaps, and a moulded GRP (glassfibre-reinforced plastic) fuselage. The "butterfly" tail combines the functions of elevators and rudder, a mixing unit in the control circuit combining pitch and yaw commands. It is anticipated that exports of the ATL will commence in 1986, after certification to FAR 23 standards. Some flight testing was conducted during 1983 with the JPX engine temporarily replaced by a Volkswagen engine.

ROBIN ATL

Dimensions: Span, 33 ft 3½ in (10,15 m); length, 21 ft 8 in (6,60 m); wing area, 129·2 sq ft (12,00 m²).

ROCKWELL B-1B

Country of Origin: USA.

Type: Strategic bomber and cruise missile carrier.

Power Plant: Four 30,750 lb st (13 948 kgp) General Electric F101-GE-102 turbofans.

Performance: Max speed (clean condition), 792 mph (1 275 km/h) or Mach 1·2 at 40,000 ft (12 190 m); low-level penetration speed, 610 mph (980 km/h) or Mach 0·8.

Weights: Empty, 179,985 lb (81 641 kg); max take-off, 477,000 lb (216 367 kg).

Accommodation: Flight crew of four comprising pilot, co-pilot and offensive and defensive systems operators.

Armament: Eight AGM-86B cruise missiles and 12 AGM-69 defence-suppression missiles internally, plus 12–14 AGM-86Bs externally, or 84 500-lb (227-kg) Mk 82 bombs internally, plus 44 externally, or 24 free-falling B-61 nuclear bombs, plus 14 externally.

Status: First contract placed 20 January 1982 in programme entailing manufacture of 100 B-1Bs, the first being scheduled for flight test December 1984. Fifteenth B-1B to be delivered mid-1986, with production attaining four monthly by late 1986 and 100th delivered by April 1988.

Notes: The B-1B is a derivative of the Mach 2·2 B-1, first of four prototypes of which flew 23 December 1974. A 347-flight, 1,895-hour test programme was completed with these aircraft on 30 April 1981. The B-1B will have reduced speed capability by comparison with the B-1, being optimised for low-level penetration. After modification to incorporate many of the B-1B features, the second B-1 prototype (illustrated above) resumed flight testing on 23 March 1983, and will be joined in July 1984 by the fourth B-1 prototype which will incorporate the remainder of the B-1B features.

ROCKWELL B-1B

Dimensions: Span (15 deg), 136 ft 8½ in (41,67 m), (67·5 deg), 78 ft 2½ in (23,84 m); length, 146 ft 8 in (44,70 m); height, 33 ft 7¼ in (10,24 m); wing area (approx), 1,950 sq ft (181,2 m²).

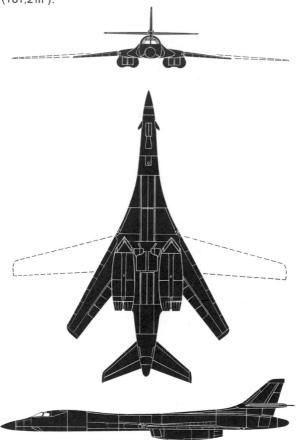

SAAB (JA) 37 VIGGEN

Country of Origin: Sweden.

Type: Single-seat all-weather interceptor fighter with second-ary strike capability.

Power Plant: One 16,200 lb st (7 350 kgp) dry and 28,110 lb st (12 750 kgp) reheat Volvo Flygmotor RM 8B turbofan.

Performance: Max speed (with four AAMs), 838 mph (1 350 km/h) or Mach 1·1 at sea level, 1,255–1,365 mph (2 020–2 195 km/h) or Mach 1·9–2·1 at 36,090 ft (11 000 m); time (from brakes off) to 32,810 ft (10 000 m), 1·4 min; tactical radius (Mach 2·0 interceptor mission), 250 mls (400 km), (counterair mission with centreline drop tank and 3,000 lb/1 360 kg of external ordnance), 650 mls (1 046 km) HI-LO-HI, 300 mls (480 km) LO-LO-LO.

Weights: Empty (approx), 26,895 lb (12 200 kg); combat (cannon armament and half fuel), 33,070 lb (15 000 kg), (with four AAMs), 37,040 lb (16 800 kg); max take-off, 49,600 lb (22 500 kg).

Armament: One 30-mm Oerlikon KCA cannon and (inter-cept) two Rb 72 Sky Flash and two (or four) Rb 24 Sidewinder AAMs, or (interdiction) 13,227 lb (6 000 kg) of external ord-nance.

Status: First of four JA 37 prototypes (modified from AJ 37 airframes) flown June 1974, with fifth and definitive prototype flown 15 December 1975. First production JA 37 flown on 4 November 1977, and total of 149 JA 37s (of 329 Viggens of all types) being produced for Swedish Air Force with some 90 delivered by beginning of 1984 and final deliveries scheduled for 1985.

Notes: The JA 37 is an optimised interceptor derivative of the AJ 37 attack aircraft (see 1973 edition).

SAAB (JA) 37 VIGGEN

Dimensions: Span, 34 ft 9¼ in (10,60 m); length (excluding probe) 50 ft 8¼ in (15,45 m); height, 19 ft 4¼ in (5,90 m); wing area (including foreplanes), 561·88 sq ft (52,20 m²).

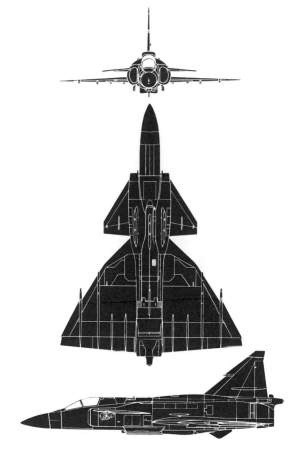

SAAB-FAIRCHILD 340

Countries of Origin: Sweden and USA.
Type: Regional airliner and corporate transport.
Power Plant: Two 1,600 shp General Electric CT7-7E or (corporate version) 1,630 shp CT7-5A turboprops.
Performance: (Regional airliner) Max cruise speed, 315 mph (508 km/h) at 15,000 ft (4 570 m); long-range cruise, 243 mph (391 km/h) at 25,000 ft (7 620 m); max climb, 1,800 ft/min (9,14 m/sec); service ceiling, 25,000 ft (7 620 m); range (max passengers) with allowances for 115-mile diversion and 45 min hold, 1,048 mls (1 686 km), (max fuel), 2,015 mls (3 243 km).
Weights: Typical operational empty, 17,000 lb (7 711 kg); max take-off, 27,000 lb (12 247) kg).
Accommodation: Flight crew of two and standard regional airliner arrangement for 35 passengers three-abreast with offset aisle. Standard corporate arrangement providing 16 seats with various options.
Status: First prototype flown 25 January 1983, with second and third prototypes following on 11 May and 25 August 1983 respectively. First production aircraft flown mid-January 1984, with certification scheduled for April 1984, with first US airline configured aircraft to be delivered (to Comair) during the following month and first corporate version being delivered (to the Mellon Bank) in July 1984. Twenty-four to be delivered by end of 1984, with 50 being completed in following years. Between 90 and 100 on firm order at beginning of 1984.
Notes: The Saab-Fairchild 340 is the subject of a joint programme between Saab-Scania (Sweden) and Fairchild (USA) with development costs shared 65-35 between the Swedish and US partners. Manufacture of the fuselage and final assembly is undertaken by Saab-Scania, the wing, tail surfaces and engine nacelles being produced by Fairchild. Included among those ordered by the beginning of 1984, were 24 of the corporate version.

SAAB-FAIRCHILD 340

Dimensions: Span, 70 ft 4 in (21,44 m); length, 64 ft 9 in (19,72 m); height, 22 ft 6 in (6,87 m); wing area, 450 sq ft (41,81 m²).

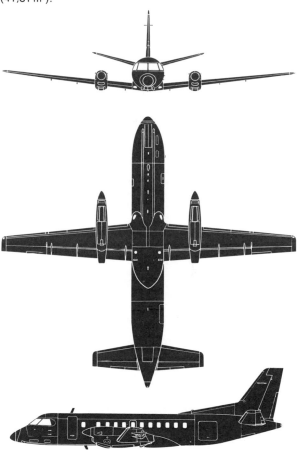

SEPECAT JAGUAR INTERNATIONAL

Countries of Origin: United Kingdom and France.
Type: Single-seat tactical strike fighter.
Power Plant: Two 5,520 lb st (2 504 kgp) dry and 8,400 lb st (3 811 kgp) reheat Rolls-Royce/Turboméca RT172-58 Adour 811 turbofans.
Performance: Max speed, 820 mph (1 320 km/h) or Mach 1·1 at sea level, 1,057 mph (1 700 km/h) or Mach 1·6 at 32,810 ft (10 000 m); combat radius (with external fuel), 282 mls (454 km) LO-LO-LO, 440 mls (708 km) HI-LO-HI; unrefuelled ferry range, 2,190 mls (3 524 km).
Weights: Typical empty, 15,432 lb (7 000 kg); normal loaded (clean aircraft), 24,000 lb (11 000 kg); max take-off, 34,000 lb (15 422 kg).
Armament: Two 30-mm Aden cannon and up to 10,000 lb (4 536 kg) of ordnance on five external stations. Provision for two Matra Magic AAMs on overwing stations or AIM-9P Sidewinder AAMs on underwing stations.
Status: The Jaguar International was developed jointly by British Aerospace in the UK and Dassault-Breguet in France. The first of eight Jaguar prototypes was flown on 8 September 1968, and 202 (including 37 two-seaters) of the basic version were delivered to the RAF and 200 (including 40 two-seaters) to the *Armée de l'Air*.
Notes: Although manufactured jointly with Dassault-Breguet, the Jaguar International is assembled by British Aerospace which has been responsible for supplying 12 each to Ecuador and Oman, and 40 (including five two-seaters) to India, the last of those for the last-mentioned country having been delivered in November 1982. Oman received a further 12 during 1983, delivery of 18 to Nigeria will commence mid-1984, and 76 are being assembled by HAL in India, with progressive component manufacture, the first of these having flown on 31 March 1982.

SEPECAT JAGUAR INTERNATIONAL

Dimensions: Span, 28 ft 6 in (8,69 m); length, 50 ft 11 in (15,52 m); height, 16 ft 0½ in (4,89 m); wing area, 280·3 sq ft (24,18 m²).

SHORTS SHERPA

Country of Origin: United Kingdom.
Type: Commercial freighter and utility aircraft.
Power Plant: Two 1,198 shp Pratt & Whitney (Canada) PT6A-45R turboprops.
Performance: Max cruise speed, 218 mph (352 km/h) at 10,000 ft (3 050 m); econ cruise, 181 mph (291 km/h) at 10,000 ft (3 050 m); max initial climb, 1,180 ft/min (5,59 m/sec); range (7,000-lb/3 175-kg payload and reserves), 225 mls (362 km), (5,000-lb/2 268-kg payload), 770 mls (1 239 km).
Weights: Max take-off, 22,900 lb (10 387 kg).
Accommodation: Crew of two on flight deck and provision for standard airline freight containers up to LD3 size (of which four can be carried in all-cargo configuration). Typical loads can include two LD3 containers and nine passengers or two half-ton vehicles in the Land Rover category. Optional roller conveyor system picking up on the standard seat rails.
Status: Prototype Sherpa flown on 23 December 1982.
Notes: The Sherpa is a civil freighter version of the Shorts 330-200 30-passenger transport (see 1983 edition) for which orders and options for 112 (including -100 version) had been placed by the beginning of 1984. The forward freight door and widebody hold of the 330-200 is retained by the Sherpa unchanged, but a Shorts Skyvan-type full-width rear cargo door permitting through-loading is incorporated. A fundamentally similar aircraft, the UTT (Utility Tactical Transport), is proposed, this having twin side-loading doors rather than the ramp-type rear cargo door. The UTT will have an essentially similar performance to that of the Sherpa.

SHORTS SHERPA

Dimensions: Span, 74 ft 9 in (22,78 m); length, 58 ft 0½ in (17,69 m); height, 16 ft 3 in (4,95 m); wing area, 453 sq ft (42,10 m²).

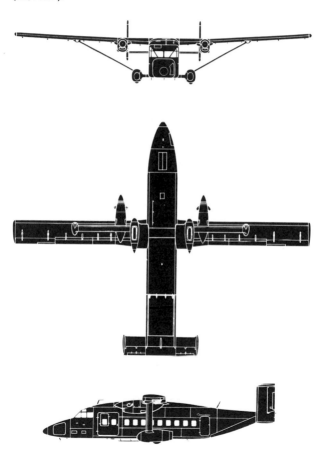

SHORTS 360

Country of Origin: United Kingdom.
Type: Regional airliner.
Power Plant: Two 1,327 shp Pratt & Whitney (Canada) PT6A-65R turboprops.
Performance: High-speed cruise, 243 mph (391 km/h) at 10,000 ft (3 050 m); range at max. cruise (with max payload and allowances for 100-mile/160-km diversion and 45 min hold), 360 mls (579 km), (with max fuel and same reserves), 860 mls (1 384 km).
Weights: Operational empty, 16,600 lb (7 530 kg); max take-off, 25,700 lb (11 657 kg).
Accommodation: Flight crew of two with standard arrangement for 36 passengers in 11 rows three-abreast. Baggage compartments in nose and aft of cabin.
Status: The prototype Shorts 360 flew for the first time on 1 June 1981, the first production aircraft following on 19 August 1982. First customer delivery (to Allegheny) on 11 November 1982, and 30 aircraft delivered by beginning of 1984, against 71 orders and options. Production rate of Shorts 360 running at three monthly from March 1984.
Notes: The Shorts 360 is a growth version of the 330 (see pages 192–3) and differs from its progenitor primarily in having a 3-ft (91-cm) cabin stretch ahead of the wing and an entirely redesigned rear fuselage and tail assembly. The fuselage lengthening permits the insertion of two additional rows of three seats in the main cabin, and the lower aerodynamic drag by comparison with the earlier aircraft contributes to a higher performance.

SHORTS 360

Dimensions: Span, 74 ft 10 in (22,81 m); length, 70ft 10in (21,59m); height, 23ft 8in (7,21 m); wing area, 454 sq ft (42,18 m²).

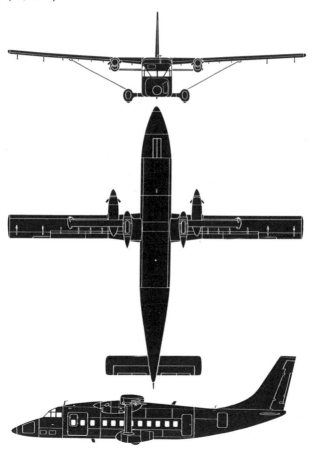

SKYFOX CORPORATION SKYFOX

Country of Origin: USA.

Type: Tandem two-seat basic and advanced trainer.

Power Plant: Two 3,700 lb st (1 680 kgp) Garrett TFE 731-3 turbofans.

Performance: Max speed, 582 mph (936 km/h) at sea level, 528 mph (850 km/h) at 40,000 ft (12 190 m) or Mach 0·80; initial climb, 10,000 ft/min (50,8 m/sec); time to 30,000 ft (9 150 m), 5 min; range (internal fuel only), 3,455 mls (5 560 km).

Weights: Empty, 8,500 lb (3 856 kg); max take-off, 14,400 lb (6 532 kg).

Status: The first of two prototypes of the Skyfox (produced by Volpar Inc) was flown on 23 August 1983. Production (from existing Lockheed T-33 airframes) is expected to be undertaken in Portugal by OGMA (Oficinas Gerais de Material Aeronautico) under contract to Skyfox Corp.

Notes: The Skyfox is a heavily modified and updated rework of the Lockheed T-33A of late 'forties vintage and of which some 1,500 are still available worldwide. Although some 70 per cent of the structural core of the T-33A is retained, the Skyfox has a new forward fuselage, extended wing root leading edges, a new lower centre fuselage, a new low-drag rear fuselage, an enlarged tail unit, winglets in place of tip-tanks and two turbofans in fuselage-side nacelles replacing the single buried centrifugal-flow turbojet. There is thus a considerable amount of new manufacture necessary, as well as the installation of new systems and sub-systems, those components that are retained being zero-timed. Current planning envisages flight development being completed in the USA with a production-conversion line being set up at Alverca by OGMA, the Portuguese Air Force having issued a letter of intent for 20 conversions and negotiations having been under way with the air arms of 12 other nations at the beginning of 1984.

SKYFOX CORPORATION SKYFOX

Dimensions: Span, 37 ft 10 in (11,83 m); length, 44 ft 0 in (13,41 m); height, 12 ft 4 in (3,76 m).

SOKO G-4 SUPER GALEB

Country of Origin: Yugoslavia.

Type: Tandem two-seat basic and advanced trainer and light strike aricraft.

Power Plant: One 4,000 lb st (1 814 kgp) Rolls-Royce Viper 632-48 turbojet.

Performance: (At 10,494 lb/4 760 kg) Max speed, 565 mph (910 km/h) at 19,685 ft (6 000 m); max climb, 5,905 ft/min (30 m/sec); time to 26,245 ft (8 000 m), 6·0 min; combat radius (at 11,442 lb/5 190 kg) with ventral gun pack and two rocket pods, 186 mls (300 km) LO-LO-LO.

Weights: Empty equipped, 7,165 lb (3 250 kg); normal loaded (training mission), 10,494 lb (4 760kg), (combat mission), 13,470 lb (6 110 kg); max overload, 13,955 lb (6 330 kg).

Armament: One 23-mm twin-barrel GSh-23L cannon in ventral pack and various external ordnance loads on four external hardpoints of 772 lb (350 kg) capacity inboard and 551 lb (250 kg) outboard.

Status: First of two prototypes flown on 17 July 1978 with second following on 18 December 1979. First of pre-series batch flown on 17 December 1980, with series production version entering Yugoslav Air Force service early 1983.

Notes: The G-4 Super Galeb (Super Gull) had been developed as a successor in Yugoslav Air Force service to the G-2A Galeb, but possessing no commonality with its predecessor other than design origin. Pre-series aircraft differed from the production model illustrated in having a conventional tail with neither dihedral nor anhedral, this being supplanted by an all-flying anhedralled tail. Like the G-2A – which was still in production in 1983 to fulfil a follow-on order for the Libyan Arab Republic Air Force – the G-4 is being offered for export.

SOKO G-4 SUPER GALEB

Dimensions: Span, 32 ft 5 in (9,88 m); length, 38 ft 11 in (11,86 m); height, 14 ft 0 in (4,28 m); wing area, 209·9 sq ft (19,50 m²).

SUKHOI SU-17 FITTER

Country of Origin: USSR.

Type: Single-seat (Fitter-C, D and H) attack and counterair aircraft, and (Fitter-F and J) multi-role fighter.

Power Plant: (Fitter-C, D and H) One 17,195 lb st (7 800 kgp) dry and 24,700 lb st (11 200 kgp) reheat Lyulka AL-21F turbojet, or (Fitter-F and J) 17,635 lb st (8 000 kgp) dry and 25,350 lb st (11 500 kgp) Tumansky R-29B turbojet.

Performance: (Estimated for Fitter-H) Max speed (short-period dash), 1,430 mph (2 300 km/h) or Mach 2·17 at 39,370 ft (12 000 m), (sustained), 808 mph (1 300 km/h) or Mach 1·06 at sea level, 1,190 mph (1 915 km/h) or Mach 1·8 at 39,370 ft (12 000 m); combat radius (drop tanks on outboard wing pylons and 4,410 lb/2 000 kg of external ordnance), 320 mls (515 km) LO-LO-LO, 530 mls (853 km) HI-LO-HI.

Weights: (Fitter-H) Max take-off, 39,022 lb (17 700 kg).

Armament: Two 30-mm NR-30 cannon and max. external ordnance load of 7,716 lb (3 500 kg).

Status: Variable-geometry derivative of fixed-geometry Su-7 (Fitter-A) first flown as technology demonstrator in 1966 as S-22I (Fitter-B). Initial series as Su-17 (Fitter-C) entered Soviet service in 1971, and subsequently supplied as the Su-20 to Algeria, Egypt, Iraq, Poland and Vietnam. Upgraded model with lengthened forward fuselage (Fitter-D) followed into Soviet service in 1976, and re-engined (R-29B) export version (Fitter-F) exported to Peru as Su-22. Extensively revised version (Fitter-H) introduced 1979, and re-engined (R-29B) export equivalent supplied to Libya (Fitter-J) as Su-22.

Notes: The Lyulka-powered Fitter-H (opposite page) and Tumansky-powered Fitter-J (illustrated above) are current production versions of the Su-17. Export versions of the Su-17 with the respective engines are referred to as Su-20 and Su-22.

SUKHOI SU-17 FITTER

Dimensions: (Estimated) Span (28 deg sweep), 45 ft 0 in (13,70 m), (68 deg sweep), 32 ft 6 in (9,90 m); length (including probe) 58 ft 3 in (17,75 m); height, 15 ft 5 in (4,70 m); wing area, 410 sq ft (38,00 m²).

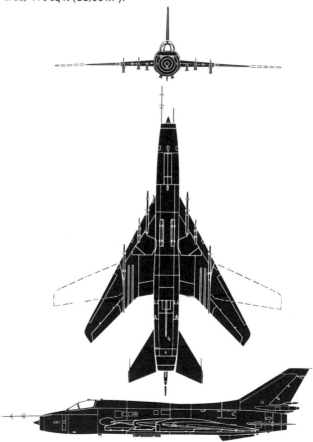

SUKHOI SU-24 (FENCER)

Country of Origin: USSR.

Type: Deep penetration interdictor and strike aircraft.

Power Plant: Two 17,635 lb st (8 000 kgp) dry and 25,350 lb st (11 500 kgp) reheat Tumansky R-29 turbofans.

Performance: (Estimated) Max. speed (clean), 915 mph (1 470 km/h) or Mach 1·2 at sea level, 1,520 mph (2 446 km/h) or Mach 2·3 above 36,000 ft (11 000 m); tactical radius (combat tanks and 4,400 lb/2 000 kg of ordnance), 1,050 mls (1 690 km) HI-LO-HI, 345 mls (555 km) LO-LO-LO.

Weights: (Estimated) Empty equipped, 41,890 lb (19 000 kg); max. take-off, 87,080 lb (39 500 kg).

Armament: One 23-mm six-barrel rotary cannon and one 30-mm cannon, and (short-range interdiction) up to 22 220-lb (100-kg) or 551-lb (250-kg) bombs, or 16 1,102-lb (500-kg) bombs. Various alternative missile loads.

Status: Prototype believed flown 1970, with initial operational status achieved late 1974. Production of approx 10 monthly as beginning of 1984, when 700–800 in service.

Notes: The first Soviet aircraft designed from the outset for interdiction and counterair missions, the Su-24 carries pilot and weapon systems operator side by side. Two versions of the SU-24 have been reported in service, these, referred to as the Fencer-A and -C, differing primarily in equipment fit.

SUKHOI SU-24 (FENCER)

Dimensions: (Estimated) Span (16 deg sweep), 56 ft 6 in (17,25 m), (68 deg sweep), 33 ft 9 in (10,30 m); length (excluding probe) 65 ft 6 in (20,00 m) height, 18 ft 0 in (5,50 m); wing area, 452 sq ft (42,00 m²).

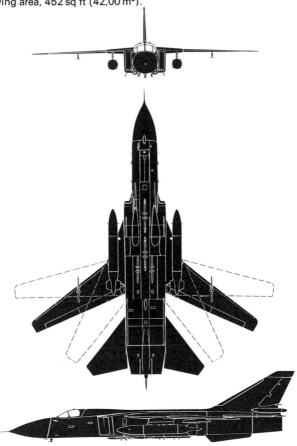

SUKHOI SU-25 (FROGFOOT)

Country of Origin: USSR.

Type: Single-seat close air support aircraft.

Power Plant: Two 11,240 lb st (5 100 kgp) Tumansky R-13-300 turbojets.

Performance: (Estimated) Max speed, 420 mph (675 km/h) at sea level, 440 mph (708 km/h) at 10,000 ft (3 050 m); service ceiling, 35,000 ft (10 670 m); combat radius (with 10,000-lb/4 535-kg warload), 300 mls (480 km) at 25,000 ft (7 620 m).

Weights: (Estimated) Max take-off, 38,000 lb (17 237 kg).

Armament: One six-barrel 30-mm rotary cannon. Ten external ordnance stations (eight wing and two fuselage) each capable of carrying a 1,102-lb (500-kg) bomb, a rocket pod or several types of anti-armour and anti-radiation missile.

Status: The Su-25 was first reported in 1980 and is believed to have entered flight test during 1977–78. Initial deliveries to the *Frontovaya Aviatsiya* are likely to have been made during 1980, and the aircraft was first deployed with an operational trials unit in Afghanistan during 1981.

Notes: The Su-25 is the Soviet equivalent of the Fairchild A-10A Thunderbolt II (see 1982 edition), and both single and two-seat versions are known to exist, the latter presumably being an operational training variant probably retaining combat capability. During operations with what is believed to be a trials unit in Afghanistan, the Su-25 has apparently been used to perfect the integration of low-level tactics of this fixed-wing aircraft with Mi-24 gunship helicopters. The Su-25 is expected to see large-scale deployment by *Frontovaya Aviatsiya* (Frontal Aviation) of the Soviet Air Forces during 1984–85.

SUKHOI SU-25 (FROGFOOT)

Dimensions: (Estimated) Span, 55 ft 0 in (16,75 m); length, 49 ft 0 in (14,95 m); height. 15 ft 0 in (4,57 m).

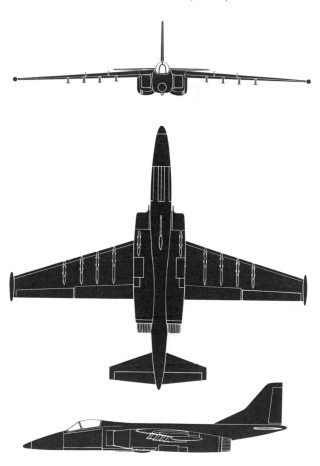

SUKHOI SU-27 (FLANKER)

Country of Origin: USSR.

Type: Single-seat multi-role fighter.

Power Plant: Two 20,000 lb st (9 070 kgp) dry and 30,000 lb st (13 610 kgp) reheat turbofans.

Performance: (Estimated) Max speed, 1,520 mph (2 445 km/h) above 36,100 ft (11 000 m), or Mach 2·3; initial climb, 60,000 ft/min (304,5 m/sec); radius (high-altitude and clean condition), 520 mls (835 km), (with eight AAMs), 405 mls (650 km), (with 12 1,100-lb/500-kg bombs), 375 mls (600 km).

Weights: (Estimated) Empty, 39,000 lb (17 690 kg); loaded (air-air mission with four AAMs and half fuel), 44,000 lb (19 960 kg); max take-off, 63,500 lb (28 800 kg).

Armament: Likely ordnance for the air-air role mix of AA-7 Apex and AA-8 Aphid air-to-air missiles, and (for the attack mission) up to 13,200 lb (5 987 kg) of bombs and air-to-surface missiles.

Status: The Su-27 has been under development since the late 'seventies, having been initially designated as Ram-K when first identified at Ramenskoye in 1977. Production is believed to have been initiated in 1980-81, and initial operational capability is expected to be achieved during 1984–85.

Notes: Possessing full dual-role (counterair and attack) capability, the Su-27 is expected to see initial deployment in a slightly later timeframe than the MiG-29, which it generally resembles in configuration while being substantially larger and heavier. The Su-27 is comparable in both size and weight to the F-15 Eagle, and is equipped with a pulse Doppler lookdown, shootdown weapons system.

SUKHOI SU-27 (FLANKER)

Dimensions: (Estimated) Span, 41 ft 0 in (12,50 m); length, 65 ft 7 in (20,00 m); wing area, 500 sq ft (46,45 m²).

TRANSALL C.160NG

Countries of Origin: France and Federal Germany.
Type: Medium-range tactical transport.
Power Plant: Two 6,100 eshp Rolls-Royce/SNECMA Tyne RTy 20 Mk 22 turboprops.
Performance: Max speed, 319 mph (513 km/h) at 16,000 ft (4 875 m); max continuous cruise, 310 mph (499 km/h) at 20,000 ft (6 100 m); econ cruise, 282 mph (454 km/h); initial climb (at 108,355 lb/49 150 kg), 1,360 ft/min (6,9 m/sec); max. range (with max. payload and reserves of five per cent and 30 min), 1,150 mls (1 850 km), (with max. fuel and 17,637 lb/8 000 kg payload), 5,500 mls (8 854 km).
Weights: Operational empty, 61,728 lb (28 000 kg); max take-off, 112,434 lb (51 000 kg).
Accommodation: Flight crew of three and up to 35,273 lb (16 000 kg) of freight, 66–88 paratroops, 93 fully-equipped troops, or up to 63 casualty stretchers and four medical attendants.
Status: First of second (relaunched) C.160 production series flown on 9 April 1981, and production was continuing at a rate of 0·7 monthly at the beginning of 1984 against orders for 25 for the *Armée de l'Air* and three for the Indonesian government, with 23 delivered, and eight to be produced during year. A further seven are to be procured by the *Armée de l'Air*.
Notes: The C.160NG is a relaunched production version of the original C.160, the first prototype of which was flown on 25 February 1963, with two further prototypes and 179 production aircraft having been built when manufacture terminated in 1972. The C.160NG embodies numerous refinements and improvements, 10 aircraft being equipped to serve as flight refuelling tankers and all having provision for in-flight refuelling. Manufacture is shared between France (Aérospatiale) and Federal Germany (MBB/VFW).

TRANSALL C.160NG

Dimensions: Span, 131 ft 3 in (40,00 m); length (excluding refuelling probe), 106 ft 3½ in (32,40 m); height, 38 ft 2 in (11,65 m); wing area, 1,723·3 sq ft (160,10 m²).

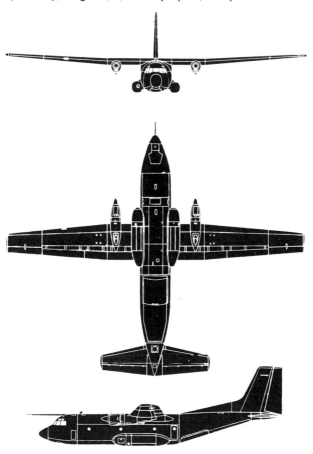

TUPOLEV TU-22M (BACKFIRE-B)

Country of Origin: USSR.

Type: Medium-range strategic bomber and maritime strike/reconnaissance aircraft.

Power Plant: Two (estimated) 33,070 lb st (15 000 kgp) dry and 46,300 lb st (21 000 kgp) reheat Kuznetsov turbofans.

Performance: (Estimated) Max speed (short-period dash), 1,265 mph (2 036 km/h) or Mach 1·91 at 39,370 ft (12 000 m), (sustained), 1,056 mph (1 700 km/h) or Mach 1·6 at 39,370 ft (12 000 m), 685 mph (1 100 km/h) or Mach 0·9 at sea level; combat radius (unrefuelled with single AS-4 ASM and high-altitude subsonic mission profile), 2,610 mls (4 200 km); max unrefuelled combat range (with 12,345 lb/5 600 kg internal ordnance), 3,420 mls (5 500 km).

Weights: (Estimated) Max take-off, 260,000 lb (118 000 kg).

Armament: Remotely-controlled tail barbette housing twin 23-mm NR-23 cannon. Internal load of free-falling weapons up to 12,345 lb (5 600 kg) or one AS-4 Kitchen inertially-guided stand-off missile housed semi-externally.

Status: Flight testing of initial prototype commenced late 1969, with pre-production series of up to 12 aircraft following in 1972–73. Initial version (Backfire-A) was built in small numbers only. Initial operational capability attained with Backfire-B in 1975–76, production rate of 30 annually being attained in 1977 and remaining constant at beginning of 1984, when 120–125 were in service with Soviet Long-range Aviation and a similar quantity with the Soviet Naval Air Force. An advanced version, the Backfire-C, with redesigned engine air intakes and presumably uprated engines has been reported under test, but its production status was uncertain at the beginning of 1984.

TUPOLEV TU-22M (BACKFIRE-B)

Dimensions: (Estimated) Span (20 deg sweep), 115 ft 0 in (35,00 m), (55 deg sweep), 92 ft 0 in (28,00 m); length, 138 ft 0 in (42,00 m); height, 29 ft 6 in (9,00 m); wing area, 1,830 sq ft (170,00 m²).

TUPOLEV (BLACKJACK-A)

Country of Origin: USSR.

Type: Long-range strategic bomber and maritime strike/reconnaissance aircraft.

Power Plant: Four 30,000 lb st (13 610 kgp) dry and 50,000 lb st (22 680 kgp) reheat turbofans.

Performance: (Estimated) Max (over-target dash) speed, 1,380 mph (2 220 km/h) at 40,000 ft (12 200 m), or Mach 2·09; range cruise, 595 mph (960 km/h) at 45,000 ft (13 720 m), or Mach 0·9; unrefuelled combat radius, 4,540 mls (7 300 km).

Weights: (Estimated) Empty, 260,000 lb (117 950 kg); max take-off, 590,000 lb (267 625 kg).

Armament: Maximum weapon load of (estimated), 36,000 lb (16 330 kg).

Status: First identified under test (at Ramenskoye) in 1979. Believed to have entered production 1982-83, with initial operational capability anticipated in 1986.

Notes: Initially known by the provisional identification designation Ram-P and a product of the Tupolev design bureau, Blackjack-A is apparently some 25 per cent larger than the Rockwell B-1B and is intended as a replacement for the intercontinental attack version of the Tu-95 Bear. It is anticipated that the Soviet Union will build a series of about 100 bombers of this type.

TUPOLEV (BLACKJACK-A)

Dimensions: (Estimated) Span (minimum sweep), 150 ft 0 in (54,00 m), (maximum sweep), 101 ft 0 in (30,75 m); length, 175 ft 0 in (53,35 m); wing area, 2,500 sq ft (232,25 m²).

YAKOVLEV YAK-36MP (FORGER-A)

Country of Origin: USSR.

Type: Shipboard VTOL air defence and strike fighter.

Power Plant: One (estimated) 17,640 lb st (8 000 kgp) lift/cruise turbojet plus two (estimated) 7,935 lb st (3 600 kgp) lift turbojets.

Performance: (Estimated) Max speed, 648 mph (1 042 km/h) or Mach 0·85 at sea level, 595 mph (956 km/h) or Mach 0·9 above 36,000 ft (10 970 m); high-speed cruise, 560 mph (900 km/h) at 20,000 ft (6 095 m); tactical radius (internal fuel and 2,000 lb/900 kg ordnance), 230 mls (370 km), HI-LO-HI, 150 mls (240 km) LO-LO-LO, (recce mission with recce pod, two drop tanks and two AAMs), 340 mls (547 km).

Weights: (Estimated) Empty equipped, 16,500 lb (7 485 kg); max take-off, 25,000 lb (11 340 kg).

Armament: Four underwing pylons with total (estimated) capacity of 2,205 lb (1 000 kg) for bombs, rockets, gun or rocket pods, or IR-homing AAMs.

Status: The Yak-36MP is believed to have flown in prototype form in 1971, and to have attained service evaluation status in 1976. At the beginning of 1984, the Yak-36MP was deployed aboard the carriers *Kiev, Minsk* and *Novorossiisk.*

Notes: The Yak-36 is unique among current service combat aircraft in that it possesses vertical take-off-and-landing capability but is incapable of performing rolling take-offs or landings. A tandem two-seat conversion trainer version (Forger-B) has an extended forward fuselage to accommodate a second cockpit, the nose being dropped to provide the two ejection seats with a measure of vertical stagger.

YAKOVLEV YAK-36MP (FORGER-A)

Dimensions: (Estimated) Span, 24 ft 7 in (7,50 m); length, 52 ft 6 in (16,00 m); height, 11 ft 0 in (3,35 m); wing area, 167 sq ft (15,50 m²).

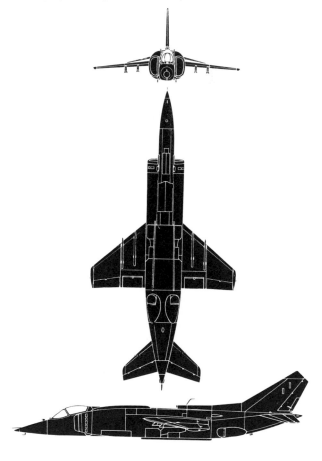

AÉROSPATIALE AS 332L SUPER PUMA

Country of Origin: France.
Type: Medium transport helicopter.
Power Plant: Two 1,755 shp Turboméca Makila turboshafts.
Performance: (At 18,080 lb/8 200 kg) Max speed, 184 mph (296 km/h); max cruise, 173 mph (278 km/h) at sea level, max. inclined climb. 1,810 ft/min (9,2 m/sec); hovering ceiling (in ground effect), 9,840 ft (3 000 m), (out of ground effect), 7,545 ft (2 300 m); range, 527 mls (850 km).
Weights: Empty, 9,635 lb (4 370 kg); normal loaded, 18,080 lb (8 200 kg); max take-off, 19,840 lb (9 000 kg).
Dimensions: Rotor diam, 49 ft 5¾ in (15,08 m); fuselage length, 48 ft 7¾ in (14,82 m).
Notes: First flown on 10 October 1980, the AS 332L is a stretched (by 2·5 ft/76 cm) version of the basic Super Puma which is being produced in civil (AS 332C) and military (AS 332B) versions. The AS 332L and M are respectively civil and military variants of the stretched model, and the AS 332F is a navalised ASW version with an overall length of 42 ft 1⅓ in (12,83 m) with rotor blades folded. Deliveries of the AS 332C began in October 1981 with the AS 332L following in December. Sixty-six Super Pumas (all versions) delivered by 30 June 1983, when production was six monthly and when 144 had been ordered. The AS 332B and C carry 20 troops and 17 passengers respectively. Eleven AS 331s have been assembled by Nurtanio in Indonesia, where more than 50 AS 332s are now being built.

AÉROSPATIALE SA 342 GAZELLE

Country of Origin: France.
Type: Five-seat light utility helicopter.
Power Plant: One 858 shp Turboméca Astazou XIVH turbo-shaft.
Performance: Max speed, 192 mph (310 km/h); max continuous cruise, 163 mph (263 km/h) at sea level; max inclined climb, 1,675 ft/min (8,5 m/sec); hovering ceiling (in ground effect), 11,970 ft (3 650 m), (out of ground effect), 9,430 ft (2 875 m); range, 469 mls (754 km) at sea level.
Weights: Empty equipped, 2,149 lb (975 kg); max take-off (normal), 4,190 lb (1 900 kg).
Dimensions: Rotor diam, 34 ft 5½ in (10,50 m); fuselage length (tail rotor included), 31 ft 2¾ in (9,53 m).
Notes: A more powerful derivative of the SA 341 (592 shp Astazou IIIA), the SA 342 has been exported to Kuwait, Iraq, Libya and other Middle Eastern countries, and may be fitted with four or six HOT missiles, a 20-mm cannon and other weapons for the anti-armour role. One hundred and ten of the French Army's (166) SA 341F Gazelles are being equipped for HOT missiles as AS 341 Ms, and 128 SA 342Ms were in process of delivery to the French Army during 1983. Versions of the lower-powered SA 341 comprise the SA 341B (British Army), SA 341C (British Navy), SA 341D (RAF), SA 341G (civil) and SA 341H (military export). Orders for the SA 341 and 342 Gazelles totalled some 1,100 by the beginning of 1984, and production was continuing in collaboration with Westland.

AÉROSPATIALE AS 350 ECUREUIL

Country of Origin: France.
Type: Six-seat light general-purpose utility helicopter.
Power Plant: (AS 350B) One 641 shp Turboméca Arriel, or (AS 350D) 615 shp Avco Lycoming LTS 101-600A2 turboshaft.
Performance: (AS 350B) Max speed, 169 mph (272 km/h) at sea level; cruise, 144 mph (232 km/h); max inclined climb, 1,555 ft/min (7,9 m/sec); hovering ceiling (in ground effect), 9,678 ft (2 950 m), (out of ground effect), 7,382 ft (2 250 m); range, 435 mls (700 km) at sea level.
Weights: Empty, 2,348 lb (1 065 kg); max take-off, 4,630 lb (2 100 kg).
Dimensions: Rotor diam, 35 ft 0¾ in (10,69 m); fuselage length (tail rotor included), 35 ft 9½ in (10,91 m).
Notes: The first Ecureuil (Squirrel) was flown on 27 June 1974 (with an LTS 101 turboshaft) and the second on 14 February 1975 (with an Arriel). The LTS 101-powered version (AS 350D) is being marketed in the USA as the AStar. By the beginning of 1984, production rate of both versions combined was running at 12–13 monthly, with more than 700 delivered. The standard Ecureuil is a six-seater and features include composite rotor blades, a so-called Starflex rotor head, simplified dynamic machinery and modular assemblies to simplify changes in the field. The AS 350D AStar version is assembled and finished by Aérospatiale Helicopter at Grand Prairie, Alberta. Two hundred Ecureuils are being assembled in Brazil.

AÉROSPATIALE AS 355F ECUREUIL 2

Country of Origin: France.
Type: Six-seat light general-purpose utility helicopter.
Power Plant: Two 420 shp Allison 250-C20F turboshafts.
Performance: Max speed, 169 mph (272 km/h) at sea level; max. cruise, 144 mph (232 km/h) at sea level; max inclined climb, 1,614 ft/min (8,2 m/sec); hovering ceiling (out of ground effect), 7,900 ft (2 410 m); service ceiling, 14,800 ft (4 510 m); range, 470 mls (756 km) at sea level.
Weights: Empty, 2,778 lb (1 260 kg); max take-off, 5,292 lb (2 400 kg).
Dimensions: Rotor diam, 35 ft 0¾ in (10,69 m); fuselage length (tail rotor included), 35 ft 9½ in (10,91 m).
Notes: Flown for the first time on 27 September 1979, the Ecureuil 2 employs an essentially similar airframe and similar dynamic components to those of the single-engined AS 350 Ecureuil (see page 218), and is intended primarily for the North American market on which it is known as the TwinStar. Deliveries of the Ecureuil 2/TwinStar commenced in July 1981, with more than 340 delivered by the beginning of 1984. From the first quarter of 1982, the production model has been the AS 355F which possesses a higher maximum take-off weight than the AS 355E that it has succeeded. The AS 355F has main rotor blades of increased chord, twin-body servo command units and two electrical generators. The AS 355E may be retrofitted to F standard. Total orders for the Ecureuil 2 worldwide exceeded 500 by the beginning of 1984, when production was 10 monthly.

AÉROSPATIALE SA 365 DAUPHIN 2

Country of Origin: France.
Type: Multi-purpose and transport helicopter.
Power Plant: Two 700 shp Turboméca Arriel 1 C turboshafts.
Performance: (SA 365N) Max speed, 190 mph (305 km/h); max continuous cruise, 173 mph (278 km/h) at sea level; max inclined climb, 1,279 ft/min (6,5 m/sec); hovering ceiling (in ground effect), 3,296 ft (1 005 m), (out of ground effect), 3,116 ft (950 m); range, 548 mls (882 km) at sea level.
Weights: Empty, 4,288 lb (1 945 kg); max take-off, 8,487 lb (3 850 kg).
Dimensions: Rotor diam, 39 ft 1½ in (11,93 m); fuselage length (including tail rotor), 37 ft 6⅓ in (11,44 m).
Notes: Flown as a prototype on 31 March 1979, the SA 365 is the latest derivative of the basic Dauphin (see 1982 edition), and is being manufactured in four versions, the 10–14-seat commercial SA 365N, the military SA 365M which can transport 13 commandos and carry eight HOT missiles, the navalised SA 365F (illustrated above) with folding rotor, Agrion radar and four AS 15TT anti-ship missiles (20 ordered by Saudi Arabia for delivery from 1983) and the SA 366G, an Avco Lycoming LTS 101-750-powered search and rescue version for the US Coast Guard as the HH-65A Seaguard. Ninety of the last version are being procured by the US Coast Guard, with completion in 1985. Production of the SA 365N is scheduled to attain eight monthly during 1984, and some 70 had been delivered by the beginning of that year, with some 430 on order.

AGUSTA A 109A MK II

Country of Origin: Italy.
Type: Eight-seat light utility helicopter.
Power Plant: Two 420 shp Allison 250-C20B turboshafts.
Performance: (At 5,402 lb/2 450 kg) Max speed, 193 mph (311 km/h); max continuous cruise, 173 mph (278 km/h); range cruise, 143 mph (231 km/h); max inclined climb rate, 1,820 ft/min (9,25 m/sec); hovering ceiling (in ground effect), 9,800 ft (2 987 m), (out of ground effect), 6,800 ft (2 073 m); max. range, 356 mls (573 km).
Weights: Empty equipped, 3,125 lb (1 418 kg); max take-off, 5,730 lb (2 600 kg).
Dimensions: Rotor diam, 36 ft 1 in (11,00 m); fuselage length, 35 ft 2½ in (10,73 m).
Notes: The A 109A Mk II is an improved model of the basic A 109A, the first of four prototypes of which flew on 4 August 1971, with customer deliveries commencing late 1976. Some 300 A 109As had been ordered by the beginning of 1984, at which time more than 220 had been delivered with production running at four–five monthly. The Mk II, which supplanted the initial model in production during 1981, has been the subject of numerous detail improvements, the transmission rating of the combined engines being increased from 692 to 740 shp, and the maximum continuous rating of each engine from 385 to 420 shp. An anti-armour version has been procured by Argentine, Libyan and Yugoslav forces. This can carry four or eight Hughes TOW anti-armour missiles.

221

AGUSTA A 129 MANGUSTA

Country of Origin: Italy.
Type: Two-seat light attack helicopter.
Power Plant: Two 915 shp Rolls-Royce Gem 2 Mk 1004D turboshafts.
Performance: (Estimated) Max speed, 173 mph (278 km/h); cruise (TOW configuration at 8,377 lb/3 800 kg), 149 mph (240 km/h) at 5,740 ft (1 750 m); max inclined climb (at 8,377 lb/3 800 kg), 2,087 ft/min (10,6 m/sec); hovering ceiling at 8,090 lb/3 670 kg), (in ground effect), 10,795 ft (3 290 m), (out of ground effect), 7,840 ft (2 390 m).
Weights: Mission, 8,080 lb (3 665 kg); max take-off, 8,377 lb (3 800 kg).
Dimensions: Rotor diam, 39 ft 0½ in (11,90 m); fuselage length, 40 ft 3¼ in (12,27 m).
Notes: The A 129 Mangusta (Mongoose) dedicated attack and anti-armour helicopter with full night/bad weather combat capability has been developed to an Italian Army requirement. The first of four flying prototypes commenced flight test on 15 September 1983, and first deliveries are scheduled for mid-1986, 67 having been funded for the Italian Army. In typical anti-armour configuration, the A 129 will be armed with eight TOW missiles to which can be added 2·75-in (7-cm) rocket launchers for suppressive fire. A more advanced version, the A 129D, has been offered to Federal Germany to meet the PAH-2 requirement.

BELL MODEL 206B JETRANGER III

Country of Origin: USA.

Type: Five-seat light utility helicopter.

Power Plant: One 420 shp Allison 250-C20J turboshaft.

Performance: (At 3,200 lb/1 451 kg) Max speed, 140 mph (225 km/h) at sea level; max cruise, 133 mph (214 km/h) at sea level; hovering ceiling (in ground effect), 12,700 ft (3 871 m), (out of ground effect), 6,000 ft (1 829 m); max range (no reserve), 360 mls (579 km).

Weights: Empty, 1,500 lb (680 kg); max take-off, 3,200 lb (1 451 kg).

Dimensions: Rotor diam, 33 ft 4 in (10,16 m); fuselage length, 31 ft 2 in (9,50 m).

Notes: Introduced in 1977, with deliveries commencing in July of that year, the JetRanger III differs from the JetRanger II which it supplanted in having an uprated engine, an enlarged and improved tail rotor mast and more minor changes. Some 5,000 commercial JetRangers had been delivered by the beginning of 1984, both commercial and military versions (including production by licensees) totalling more than 7,500. A light observation version of the JetRanger for the US Army is designated OH-58 Kiowa and a training version for the US Navy is known as the TH-57A SeaRanger. The JetRanger is built by Agusta in Italy as the AB 206, and at the beginning of 1984, Agusta was producing the JetRanger at a rate of six monthly with approximately 1,070 delivered.

BELL MODEL 206L-3 LONGRANGER III

Country of Origin: USA.

Type: Seven-seat light utility helicopter.

Power Plant: One 650 shp Allison 250-C30P turboshaft.

Performance: (At 3,900 lb/1 769 kg) Max speed, 144 mph (232 km/h); cruise, 136 mph (229 km/h) at sea level; hovering ceiling (in ground effect), 16,500 ft (5 030 m), (out of ground effect), 6,000 ft (1 830 m); range, 351 mls (565 km) at sea level.

Weights: Empty, 2,160 lb (980 kg); max take-off, 4,150 lb (1 882 kg).

Dimensions: Rotor diam, 37 ft 0 in (11,28 m); fuselage length, 33 ft 3 in (10,13 m).

Notes: The Model 206L-3 LongRanger III is a stretched and more powerful version of the Model 206B JetRanger III, with longer fuselage, increased fuel capacity, an uprated engine and a larger rotor. The LongRanger is being manufactured in parallel with the JetRanger III and initial customer deliveries commenced in October 1975, prototype testing having been initiated on 11 September 1974. The LongRanger is available with emergency flotation gear and with a 2,000-lb (907-kg) capacity cargo hook. In the aeromedical or rescue role the Long Ranger can accommodate two casualty stretchers and two ambulatory casualties. The 206L-1 LongRanger II was introduced in 1978 and the uprated LongRanger III early in 1982, and production was continuing at the beginning of 1984, with more than 800 LongRangers delivered.

BELL AH-1S HUEYCOBRA

Country of Origin: USA.

Type: Two-seat light attack helicopter.

Power Plant: One 1,800 shp Avco Lycoming T53-L-703 turboshaft.

Performance: Max speed, 172 mph (277 km/h), (TOW configuration), 141 mph (227 km/h); max inclined climb, 1,620 ft/min (8,23 m/sec); hovering ceiling TOW configuration (in ground effect), 12,200 ft (3 720 m); max range, 357 mls (574 km).

Weights: (TOW configuration) Operational empty, 6,479 lb (2 939 kg); max take-off, 10,000 lb (4 535 kg).

Dimensions: Rotor diam, 44 ft 0 in (13,41 m); fuselage length, 44 ft 7 in (13,59 m).

Notes: The AH-1S is a dedicated attack and anti-armour helicopter serving primarily with the US Army which had received 297 new-production AH-1S HueyCobras by mid-1981, plus 290 resulting from the conversion of earlier AH-1G and AH-1Q HueyCobras. Current planning calls for conversion of a further 372 AH-1Gs to AH-1S standards, and both conversion and new-production AH-1S HueyCobras are being progressively upgraded to "Modernised AH-1S" standard, the entire programme being scheduled for completion in 1985, resulting in a total of 959 "Modernised" AH-1S HueyCobras. In December 1979, one YAH-1S was flown with a four-bladed main rotor as the Model 249. The AH-1S is to be licence-built in Japan.

BELL AH-1T SEACOBRA

Country of Origin: USA.

Type: Two-seat light attack helicopter.

Power Plant: One 1,970 shp Pratt & Whitney T400-WV-402 coupled turboshaft.

Performance: (Attack configuration at 12,401 lb/5 625 kg) Max speed, 181 mph (291 km/h) at sea level; average cruise, 168 mph (270 km/h); max inclined climb, 2,190 ft/min (11,12 m/sec); hovering ceiling (out of ground effect), 5,350 ft (1 630 m); range, 276 mls (445 km).

Weights: Empty, 8,030 lb (3 642 kg); max take-off, 14,000 lb (6 350 kg).

Dimensions: Rotor diam, 48 ft 0 in (14,63 m); fuselage length, 45 ft 3 in (13,79 m).

Notes: The SeaCobra is a twin-turboshaft version of the Huey-Cobra (see page 225), the initial model for the US Marine Corps having been the AH-1J (69 delivered of which two modified as AH-1T prototypes). The AH-1T features uprated components for significantly increased payload and performance, the first example having been delivered to the US Marine Corps on 15 October 1977, and a further 56 being delivered to the service of which 23 being modified to TOW configuration. Forty-four are to be procured by the USMC during Fiscal Years 1984 and 1985. The AH-1T has a three-barrel 20-mm cannon barbette under the nose, and four stores stations under the stub wings for seven- or 19-tube launchers, Minigun pods, etc.

BELL MODEL 214ST

Country of Origin: USA.
Type: Medium transport helicopter (20 seats).
Power Plant: Two 1,625 shp (limited to combined output of 2,250 shp) General Electric CT7-2A turboshafts.
Performance: Max cruising speed, 164 mph (264 km/h) at sea level, 161 mph (259 km/h) at 4,000 ft (1 220 m); hovering ceiling (in ground effect), 12,600 ft (3 840 m), (out of ground effect), 3,300 ft (1 005 m); range (standard fuel), 460 mls (740 km).
Weights: Max take-off (internal load), 15,500 lb (7 030 kg), (external jettisonable load), 16,500 lb (7 484 kg).
Dimensions: Rotor diam, 52 ft 0 in (15,85 m); fuselage length, 50 ft 0 in (15,24 m).
Notes: The Model 214ST (Super Transport) is a significantly improved derivative of the Model 214B BigLifter (see 1978 edition), production of which was phased out early 1981, and initial customer deliveries began early 1982. The Model 214ST test-bed was first flown in March 1977, and the first of three representative prototypes (one in military configuration and two for commercial certification) commenced its test pro-gramme in August 1979. Work on an initial series of 100 heli-copters of this type commenced in 1981, with some 20 in service by the beginning of 1984. A version with wheel landing gear was certificated in March 1983, and alternative layouts are available for either 16 or 17 passengers.

BELL MODEL 222B

Country of Origin: USA.
Type: Eight/ten-seat light utility and transport helicopter.
Power Plant: Two 680 shp Avco Lycoming LTS 101-750C-1 turboshafts.
Performance: Max cruising speed, 150 mph (241 km/h) at sea level, 146 mph (235 km/h) at 8,000 ft (2 400 m); max climb, 1,730 ft/min (8,8 m/sec); hovering ceiling (in ground effect), 10,300 ft (3 135 m), (out of ground effect), 6,400 ft (1 940 m); range (no reserves), 450 mls (724 km) at 8,000 ft (2 400 m).
Weights: Empty equipped, 4,577 lb (2 076 kg); max take-off (standard configuration), 8,250 lb (3 742 kg).
Dimensions: Rotor diam, 42 ft 0 in (12,80 m); fuselage length, 39 ft 9 in (12,12 m).
Notes: The first of five prototypes of the Model 222 was flown on 13 August 1976, an initial production series of 250 helicopters of this type being initiated in 1978, with production deliveries commencing in January 1980, and some 220 delivered by beginning of 1984, when production rate was two monthly. Several versions of the Model 222 are on offer or under development, these including an executive version with a flight crew of two and five or six passengers and the so-called "offshore" model with accommodation for eight passengers and a flight crew of two. Options include interchangeable skids. The Model 222B has a larger main rotor and uprated power plant, a utility version, the Model 222UT, having been certificated mid 1983.

BELL MODEL 412

Country of Origin: USA.
Type: Fifteen-seat utility transport helicopter.
Power Plant: One 1,800 shp Pratt & Whitney PT6T-3B-1 turboshaft.
Performance: Max speed, 149 mph (240 km/h) at sea level; cruise, 143 mph (230 km/h) at sea level, 146 mph (235 km/h) at 5,000 ft (1 525 m); hovering ceiling (in ground effect), 10,800 ft (3 290 m), (out of ground effect), 7,100 ft (2 165 m) at 10,500 lb/4 763 kg; max. range, 282 mls (454 km), (with auxiliary tanks), 518 mls (834 km).
Weights: Empty equipped, 6,070 lb (2 753 kg); max take-off, 11,500 lb (5 216 kg).
Dimensions: Rotor diam, 46 ft 0 in (14,02 m); fuselage length, 41 ft 8½ in (12,70 m).
Notes: The Model 412, flown for the first time in August 1979, is an updated Model 212 (production of which was continuing at the beginning of 1984) with a new-design four-bladed rotor, a shorter rotor mast assembly, and uprated engine and transmission systems, giving more than twice the life of the Model 212 units. Composite rotor blades are used and the rotor head incorporates elastomeric bearings and dampers to simplify moving parts. An initial series of 200 helicopters was laid down with customer deliveries commencing February 1981. Licence manufacture is undertaken by Agusta in Italy, a military version being designated AB 412 Griffon, and is also to be undertaken by Nurtanio in Indonesia.

BOEING VERTOL 234 CHINOOK

Country of Origin: USA.
Type: Commercial transport helicopter.
Power Plant: Two 4,075 shp Avco Lycoming AL 5512 turboshafts.
Performance: Max cruising speed (at 47,000 lb/21 318 kg), 167 mph (269 km/h) at 2,000 ft (610 m); range cruise, 155 mph (250 km/h); max inclined climb, 1,350 ft/min (6,8 m/sec); hovering ceiling (in ground effect), 9,150 ft (2 790 m), (out of ground effect), 4,900 ft (1 495 m); range (44 passengers and 45 min reserves), 627 mls (1 010 km), (max. fuel), 852 mls (1 371 km).
Weights: Empty, 24,449 lb (11 090 kg); max take-off, 47,000 lb (21 318 kg).
Dimensions: Rotor diam (each), 60 ft 0 in (18,29 m); fuselage length, 52 ft 1 in (15,87 m).
Notes: Possessing an airframe based on the latest Model 414 military Chinook (see opposite), the Model 234 has been developed specifically for commercial purposes and two basic versions are offered, a long-range model described above and a utility model with fuel tank-housing side fairings removed. The first Model 234 was flown on 19 August 1980, certification being obtained mid-1981 and the first deliveries (to British Airways Helicopters) followed during the course of the year, primarily for North Sea oil rig support, six being delivered. Two were delivered to Helikopter Service of Norway during 1983, when two were also delivered to Arco Alaska.

BOEING VERTOL 414 CHINOOK

Country of Origin: USA.
Type: Medium transport helicopter.
Power Plant: Two 3,750 shp Avco Lycoming T55-L-712 turboshafts.
Performance: (At 45,400 lb/20 593 kg) Max speed, 146 mph (235 km/h) at sea level; average cruise, 131 mph (211 km/h); max inclined climb, 1,380 ft/min (7,0 m/sec); service ceiling, 8,400 ft (2 560 m); max. ferry range, 1,190 mls (1 915 km).
Weights: Empty, 22,591 lb (10 247 kg); max take-off, 50,000 lb (22 680 kg).
Dimensions: Rotor diam (each), 60 ft 0 in (18,29 m); fuselage length, 51 ft 0 in (15,55 m).
Notes: The Model 414 as supplied to the RAF as the Chinook HC Mk 1 combines some features of the US Army's CH-47D (see 1980 edition) and features of the Canadian CH-147, but with provision for glassfibre/carbonfibre rotor blades. The first of 33 Chinook HC Mk 1s for the RAF was flown on 23 March 1980 and accepted on 2 December 1980, with deliveries continuing through 1981, three more being ordered in 1982 and five in 1983. The RAF version can accommodate 44 troops and has three external cargo hooks. During 1981, Boeing Vertol initiated the conversion to essentially similar CH-47D standards a total of 436 CH-47As, Bs and Cs, and this programme is continuing throughout 1984. Licence manufacture of the Chinook is undertaken in Italy. Illustrated is one of three Model 414s delivered to Spain in 1982.

HUGHES 500MD DEFENDER II

Country of Origin: USA.

Type: Light gunship and multi-role helicopter.

Power Plant: One 420 shp Allison 250-C20B turboshaft.

Performance: (At 3,000 lb/1 362 kg) Max speed, 175 mph (282 km/h) at sea level; cruise, 160 mph (257 km/h) at 4,000 ft (1 220 m); max inclined climb, 1,920 ft/min (9,75 m/sec); hovering ceiling (in ground effect), 8,800 ft (2 682 m), (out of ground effect), 7,100 ft (2 164 m); max range, 263 mls (423 km).

Weights: Empty, 1,295 lb (588 kg); max take-off (internal load), 3,000 lb (1 362 kg), (with external load), 3,620 lb (1 642 kg).

Dimensions: Rotor diam, 26 ft 5 in (8,05 m); fuselage length, 21 ft 5 in (6,52 m).

Notes: The Defender II multi-mission version of the Model 500MD was introduced mid-1980 for 1982 delivery, and features a Martin Marietta rotor mast-top sight, a General Dynamics twin-Stinger air-to-air missile pod, an underfuselage 30-mm chain gun and a pilot's night vision sensor. The Defender II can be rapidly reconfigured for anti-armour target designation, anti-helicopter, suppressive fire and transport roles. The Model 500MD TOW Defender (carrying four tube-launched optically-tracked wire-guided anti-armour missiles) is currently in service with Israel (30), South Korea (45) and Kenya (15). Production of the 500 was 15 monthly at beginning of 1984.

HUGHES 530E

Country of Origin: USA.

Type: Five-seat light utility helicopter.

Power Plant: One 650 shp Allison 250-C30 turboshaft.

Performance: Max cruise speed, 155 mph (250 km/h) at sea level, econ cruise, 150 mph (241 km/h) at 5,000 ft (1 525 m); max inclined climb, 1,780 ft/min (9,04 m/sec); hovering ceiling (in ground effect), 12,000 ft (3 660 m), (out of ground effect), 9,600 ft (2 925 m); range, 269 mls (434 km) at 5,000 ft (1 525 m).

Weights: Max take-off, 3,100 lb (1 406 kg).

Dimensions: Rotor diam, 27 ft 6 in (8,38 m); fuselage length, 23 ft 2½ in (7,07 m).

Notes: The Model 530 is the "hot and high" variant of the Model 500E (see 1983 edition) which is characterised by a longer, recontoured nose compared with the preceding Model 500D, offering increased leg room for front seat occupants and a 12 per cent increase in headroom for rear seat passengers. The principal difference between the Models 500E and 530 is the power plant, the former having a 520 shp 250-C20B. The Model 500E was flown on 28 January 1982, and was certificated in November 1982, and the Model 530 was flown in October 1982, with certification following in July 1983. Customer deliveries of the lower-powered helicopter commenced in November 1982, and of the higher-powered version late 1983, both types being manufactured in parallel.

HUGHES AH-64 APACHE

Country of Origin: USA.
Type: Tandem two-seat attack helicopter.
Power Plant: Two 1,690 shp General Electric T700-GE-701 turboshafts.
Performance: Max speed, 191 mph (307 km/h); cruise, 179 mph (288 km/h); max inclined climb, 3,200 ft/min (16,27 m/sec); hovering ceiling (in ground effect), 14,600 ft (4 453 m), (outside ground effect), 11,800 ft (3 600 m); service ceiling, 8,000 ft (2 400 m); max range, 424 mls (682 km).
Weights: Empty, 9,900 lb (4 490 kg); primary mission, 13,600 lb (6 169 kg); max take-off, 17,400 lb (7 892 kg).
Dimensions: Rotor diam, 48 ft 0 in (14,63 m); fuselage length, 48 ft 1⅞ in (14,70 m).
Notes: Winning contender in the US Army's AAH (Advanced Attack Helicopter) contest, the YAH-64 flew for the first time on 30 September 1975. Two prototypes were used for the initial trials, the first of three more with fully integrated weapons systems commenced trials on 31 October 1979, a further three following in 1980. Planned total procurement comprises 515 AH-64s through 1989, with 59 ordered by beginning of 1984, and a peak production rate of 12 monthly, planned deliveries, having commenced March 1984. The AH-64 is armed with a single-barrel 30-mm gun based on the chain-driven bolt system and suspended beneath the forward fuselage, and eight BGM-71A TOW or 16 Hellfire laser-seeking missiles may be carried.

KAMOV KA-25 (HORMONE A)

Country of Origin: USSR.
Type: Shipboard anti-submarine warfare helicopter.
Power Plant: Two 900 shp Glushenkov GTD-3 turboshafts.
Performance: (Estimated) Max speed, 130 mph (209 km/h); normal cruise, 120 mph (193 km/h); max range, 400 mls (644 km); service ceiling, 11,000 ft (3 353 m).
Weights: (Estimated) Empty, 10,500 lb (4 765 kg); max take-off, 16,500 lb (7 484 kg).
Dimensions: Rotor diam (each), 51 ft 7½ in (15,74 m); approx. fuselage length, 35 ft 6 in (10,82 m).
Notes: Possessing a basically similar airframe to that of the Ka-25K (see 1973 edition) and employing a similar self-contained assembly comprising rotors, transmission, engines and auxiliaries, the Ka-25 serves with the Soviet Navy primarily in the ASW role but is also employed in the utility and transport roles. The ASW Ka-25 serves aboard the helicopter cruisers *Moskva* and *Leningrad*, and the carriers *Kiev* and *Minsk*, as well as with shore-based units. A search radar installation is mounted in a nose randome, but other sensor housings and antennae differ widely from helicopter to helicopter. There is no evidence that externally-mounted weapons may be carried. Each landing wheel is surrounded by an inflatable pontoon surmounted by inflation bottles. The Hormone-A is intended for ASW operations, the Hormone-B is used for over-the-horizon missile targeting, and the Hormone-C is a utility transport with operational equipment and weapons deleted.

KAMOV KA-32 (HELIX)

Country of Origin: USSR.
Type: Shipboard anti-submarine warfare helicopter.
Power Plant: Two (approx) 1,500-1,700 shp Glushenkov GTD-3BM turboshafts.
Performance: (Estimated) Max speed, 150 mph (241 km/h) at sea level; normal cruise, 130 mph (209 km/h); max range, 600 mls (965 km); range with 11,023 lb (5 000 kg) payload, 112 mls (180 km).
Weights: (Estimated) Normal loaded, 20,000-21,000 lb (9 070-9 525 kg).
Dimensions: (Estimated) Rotor diam (each), 55 ft (16,75 m); fuselage length, 36 ft 1 in (11,00 m).
Notes: Retaining the pod-and-boom fuselage configuration and superimposed co-axial rotor arrangement of the Ka-25 Hormone (see page 235), the Ka-32 was first seen during Zapad-81 exercises held by WarPac forces in the Baltic in September 1981, and is believed to have flown in prototype form in 1979–80. Developed in both shipboard ASW and civil freight transportation versions simultaneously, the Ka-32 is larger and more powerful than the preceding Kamov helicopter which it is presumably intended to supplant in Soviet Naval service, its greater internal capacity suggesting that an alternative mission to ASW may be that of assault troop transport for operation from *Berezina*-class replenishment ships. The Ka-32 would appear suitable as a replacement for both Hormone-B and Hormone-C versions of the Ka-25.

MBB BO 105L

Country of Origin: Federal Germany.
Type: Five/six-seat light utility helicopter.
Power Plant: Two 550 shp Allison 250-C28C turboshafts.
Performance: Max speed, 168 mph (270 km/h) at sea level; max. cruise, 157 mph (252 km/h) at sea level; max climb, 1,970 ft/min (10 m/sec); hovering ceiling (in ground effect), 13,120 ft (4 000 m), (out of ground effect), 11,280 ft (3 440 m); range, 286 mls (460 km).
Weights: Empty, 2,756 lb (1 250 kg); max take-off, 5,291 lb (2 400 kg), (with external load), 5,512 lb (2 500 kg).
Dimensions: Rotor diam, 32 ft 3½ in (9,84 m); fuselage length, 28 ft 1 in (8,56 m).
Notes: The BO 105L is a derivative of the BO 105CB (see 1979 edition) with uprated transmission and more powerful turboshaft for "hot-and-high" conditions. It is otherwise similar to the BO 105CBS Twin Jet II (420 shp Allison 250-C20B) which was continuing in production at the beginning of 1984, when some 850 BO 105s (all versions) had been delivered and production was running at 10–12 monthly, and licence assembly was being undertaken in Indonesia, the Philippines and Spain. Deliveries to the Federal German Army of 227 BO 105M helicopters for liaison and observation tasks commenced late 1979, and deliveries of 212 HOT-equipped BO 105s for the anti-armour role began on 4 December 1980. The latter have uprated engines and transmission systems.

MBB-KAWASAKI BK 117

Countries of Origin: Federal Germany and Japan.
Type: Multi-purpose eight-to-twelve-seat helicopter.
Power Plant: Two 600 shp Avco Lycoming LTS 101-650B-1 turboshafts.
Performance: Max speed, 171 mph (275 km/h) at sea level; cruise, 164 mph (264 km/h) at sea level; max climb, 1,970 ft/min (10 m/sec); hovering ceiling (in ground effect), 13,450 ft (4100 m), (out of ground effect), 10,340 ft (3150 m); range (max. payload), 339 mls (545,4 km).
Weights: Empty, 3,351 lb (1 520 kg); max take-off, 6,173 lb (2 800 kg).
Dimensions: Rotor diam, 36 ft 1 in (11,00 m); fuselage length, 32 ft 5 in (9,88 m).
Notes: The BK 117 is a co-operative development between Messerschmitt-Bölkow-Blohm and Kawasaki, the first of two flying prototypes commencing its flight test programme on 13 June 1979 (in Germany), with the second following on 10 August (in Japan). A decision to proceed with series production was taken in 1980, with first flying on 24 December 1981, and production deliveries commencing first quarter of 1983. MBB is responsible for the main and tail rotor systems, tail unit and hydraulic components, while Kawasaki is responsible for production of the fuselage, undercarriage, transmission and some other components. Licence manufacture of the BK 117 is being undertaken by Nurtanio in Indonesia with deliveries to commence in 1985.

MIL MI-8 (HIP)

Country of Origin: USSR.
Type: Assault transport helicopter.
Power Plant: Two 1,700 shp Isotov TV2-117A turboshafts.
Performance: Max speed, 161 mph (260 km/h) at 3,280 ft
(1 000 m), 155 mph (250 km/h) at sea level; max cruise,
140 mph (225 km/h); hovering ceiling (in ground effect),
6,233 ft (1 900 m), (out of ground effect), 2,625 ft (800 m);
range (standard fuel), 290 mls (465 km).
Weights: (Hip-C) Empty, 14,603 lb (6 624 kg); normal
loaded, 24,470 lb (11 100 kg); max take-off, 26,455 lb
(12 000 kg).
Dimensions: Rotor diam, 69 ft 10¼ in (21,29 m); fuselage
length, 60 ft 0¾ in (18,31 m).
Notes: Currently being manufactured at a rate of 700–800
annually, with more than 7,500 delivered for civil and military
use since its debut in 1961, the Mi-8 is numerically the most
important Soviet helicopter. Current military versions include
the Hip-C basic assault transport, the Hip-D and -G with additional antennae and podded equipment for airborne communications, the Hip-E and the Hip-F, the former carrying up to six
rocket pods and four Swatter IR-homing anti-armour missiles,
and the latter carrying six Sagger wire-guided anti-armour missiles, and the Hip-J and -K ECM variants. The Mi-8 can accommodate 24 troops or 12 stretchers, and most have a 12,7-mm
machine gun in the nose. An enhanced version, the Mi-17, is
described on page 241.

MIL MI-14 (HAZE-A)

Country of Origin: USSR.
Type: Amphibious anti-submarine helicopter.
Power Plant: Two 1,900 shp Isotov TV-3 turboshafts.
Performance: (Estimated) Max speed, 143 mph (230 km/h); max cruise, 130 mph (210 km/h); hovering ceiling (in ground effect), 5,250 ft (1 600 m), (out of ground effect), 2,295 ft (700 m); tactical radius, 124 mls (200 km).
Weights: (Estimated) Max take-off, 26,455 lb (12 000 kg).
Dimensions: Rotor diam, 69 ft 10¼ in (21,29 m); fuselage length, 59 ft 7 in (18,15 m).
Notes: The Mi-14 amphibious anti-submarine warfare helicopter, which serves with shore-based elements of the Soviet Naval Air Force, is a derivative of the Mi-8 (see page 239) with essentially similar power plant and dynamic components, and much of the structure is common between the two helicopters. New features include the boat-type hull, outriggers which, housing the retractable lateral twin-wheel undercarriage members, incorporate water rudders, a search radar installation beneath the nose and a sonar "bird" beneath the tailboom root. The Haze-B is a version of the Mi-14 used for the mine countermeasures task. It may be assumed that the Mi-14 possesses a weapons bay for ASW torpedoes, nuclear depth charges and other stores. This amphibious helicopter reportedly entered service in 1975 and about 120 were in Soviet Navy service by the beginning of 1984, other recipients being Bulgaria and Libya.

MIL MI-17

Country of Origin: USSR.

Type: Medium transport helicopter.

Power Plant: Two 1,900 shp Isotov TV3-117MT turboshafts.

Performance: (At 28,660 lb/13 000 kg) Max speed, 162 mph (260 km/h); max continuous cruise, 149 mph (240 km/h) at sea level; hovering ceiling (at 24,250 lb/11 000 kg out of ground effect), 5,800 ft (1 770 m); max range, 590 mls (950 km).

Weights: Empty, 15,652 lb (7 100 kg); normal loaded, 24,250 lb (11 000 kg); max take-off, 28,660 lb (13 000 kg).

Dimensions: Rotor diam, 69 ft 10¼ in (21,29 m); fuselage length, 60 ft 5¼ in (18,42 m).

Notes: The Mi-17 medium-lift helicopter is essentially a more powerful and modernised derivative of the late fifties technology Mi-8 (see page 239). The airframe and rotor are fundamentally unchanged, apart from some structural reinforcement of the former, but higher-performance turboshafts afford double the normal climb rate and out-of-ground-effect hover ceiling of the earlier helicopter, and increase permissible maximum take-off weight. The Mi-17 has a crew of two–three and can accommodate 24 passengers, 12 casualty stretchers or up to 8,818 lb (4 000 kg) of freight. The TV3-117 turboshafts utilised by the Mi-17 are installed in late production versions of the military Mi-8 (eg, the Hip-H). Externally, the Mi-17 is virtually indistinguishable from its precursor, the Mi-8, apart from marginally shorter engine nacelles and portside tail rotor.

MIL MI-24 (HIND-D)

Country of Origin: USSR.

Type: Assault and anti-armour helicopter.

Power Plant: Two 2,200 shp Isotov TV3-117 turboshafts.

Performance: (Estimated) Max speed, 170–180 mph (273–290 km/h) at 3,280 ft (1 000 m); max cruise, 145 mph (233 km/h); max inclined climb rate, 3,000 ft/min (15,24 m/sec).

Weights: (Estimated) Normal take-off, 22,000 lb (10 000 kg).

Dimensions: (Estimated) Rotor diam, 55 ft 0 in (16,76 m); fuselage length, 55 ft 6 in (16,90 m).

Notes: By comparison with the Hind-A version of the Mi-24 (see 1977 edition), the Hind-D embodies a redesigned forward fuselage and is optimised for the gunship role, having tandem stations for the weapons operator (in nose) and pilot. The Hind-D can accommodate eight fully-equipped troops, has a barbette-mounted four-barrel rotary-type 12,7-mm cannon beneath the nose and can carry up to 2,800 lb (1 275 kg) of ordnance externally, including four AT-2 Swatter IR-homing anti-armour missiles and four pods each with 32 57-mm rockets. It has been exported to Afghanistan, Algeria, Bulgaria, Cuba, Czechoslovakia, East Germany, Hungary, Iraq, Libya, Poland and South Yemen. The Hind-E is similar but has provision for four laser-homing tube-launched Spiral anti-armour missiles, may be fitted with a twin-barrel 23-mm cannon on the starboard side of the fuselage and embodies some structural hardening, steel and titanium being substituted for aluminium in certain critical components.

MIL MI-26 (HALO)

Country of Origin: USSR.
Type: Military and commercial heavy-lift helicopter.
Power Plant: Two 11,400 shp Lotarev D-136 turboshafts.
Performance: Max speed, 183 mph (295 km/h); normal cruise, 158 mph (255 km/h); hovering ceiling (in ground effect), 14,765 ft (4 500 m), (out of ground effect), 5,905 ft (1 800 m); range (at 109,127 lb/49 500 kg), 310 mls (500 km), (at 123,457 lb/56 000 kg), 497 mls (800 km).
Weights: Empty, 62,169 lb (28 200 kg); normal load, 109,227 lb (49 500 kg); max take-off, 123,457 lb (56 000 kg).
Dimensions: Rotor diam, 104 ft 11⅞ in (32,00 m); fuselage length (nose to tail rotor), 110 ft 7¾ in (33,73 m).
Notes: The heaviest and most powerful helicopter ever flown, the Mi-26 first flew as a prototype on 14 December 1977, production of pre-series machines commencing in 1980, and preparations for full-scale production having begun in 1981. Featuring an innovative eight-bladed main rotor and carrying a flight crew of five, the Mi-26 has a max. internal payload of 44,090 lb (20 000 kg). The freight hold is larger than that of the fixed-wing Antonov An-12 transport and at least 70 combat-equipped troops or 40 casualty stretchers can be accommodated. Although allegedly developed to a civil requirement, the primary role of the Mi-26 is obviously military and the Soviet Air Force achieved initial operational capability with the series version late 1983. During the course of 1982, the Mi-26 established new international payload-to-height records.

SIKORSKY CH-53E SUPER STALLION

Country of Origin: USA.
Type: Amphibious assault transport helicopter.
Power Plant: Three 4,380 shp General Electric T64-GE-415 turboshafts.
Performance: (At 56,000 lb/25 400 kg) Max speed, 196 mph (315 km/h) at sea level; cruise, 173 mph (278 km/h) at sea level; max. inclined climb, 2,750 ft/min (13,97 m/sec); hovering ceiling (in ground effect), 11,550 ft (3 520 m), (out of ground effect), 9,500 ft (2 895 m); range, 1,290 mls (2 075 km).
Weights: Empty, 33,226 lb (15 071 kg); max take-off, 73,500 lb (33 339 kg).
Dimensions: Rotor diam, 79 ft 0 in (24,08 m); fuselage length, 73 ft 5 in (22,38 m).
Notes: The CH-53E is a growth version of the CH-53D Sea Stallion (see 1974 edition) embodying a third engine, an uprated transmission system, a seventh main rotor blade and increased rotor diameter. The first of two prototypes was flown on 1 March 1974, and the first of two pre-production examples followed on 8 December 1975, successive production orders totalling 75 helicopters to be divided between the US Navy and US Marine Corps by beginning of 1984, against total requirement for 160 through 1992. The CH-53E can accommodate up to 55 troops in a high-density seating arrangement. Fleet deliveries began mid-1981, and the first pre-production example of the MH-53E mine countermeasures version, 57 of which are required by the US Navy, flew September 1983.

SIKORSKY S-70 (UH-60A) BLACK HAWK

Country of Origin: USA.

Type: Tactical transport helicopter.

Power Plant: Two 1,543 shp General Electric T700-GE-700 turboshafts.

Performance: Max speed, 224 mph (360 km/h) at sea level; cruise, 166 mph (267 km/h); vertical climb rate, 450 ft/min (2,28 m/sec); hovering ceiling (in ground effect), 10,000 ft (3 048 m), (out of ground effect), 5,800 ft (1 758 m); endurance, 2·3-3·0 hrs.

Weights: Design gross, 16,500 lb (7 485 kg); max take-off, 22,000 lb (9 979 kg).

Dimensions: Rotor diam, 53 ft 8 in (16,23 m); fuselage length, 50 ft 0¾ in (15,26 m).

Notes: The Black Hawk was winner of the US Army's UTTAS (Utility Tactical Transport Aircraft System) contest. The first of three YUH-60As was flown on 17 October 1974, and a company-funded fourth prototype flew on 23 May 1975. The Black Hawk is primarily a combat assault squad carrier, accommodating 11 fully-equipped troops. Variants under development at the beginning of 1984 were the EH-60A ECM model, and the HH-60D, HH-60E Night Hawk rescue helicopters. The USAF is expected to procure 69 HH-60Ds and 86-60Es, the latter having reduced capability by comparison with the former. The first production deliveries of the UH-60A to the US Army were made in June 1979, with some 470 delivered by beginning of 1984 against requirement for 1,107.

SIKORSKY S-70L (SH-60B) SEA HAWK

Country of Origin: USA.

Type: Shipboard multi-role helicopter.

Power Plant: Two 1,690 shp General Electric T700-GE-401 turboshafts.

Performance: (At 20,244 lb/9 183 kg) Max speed, 167 mph (269 km/h) at sea level; max cruising speed, 155 mph (249 km/h) at 5,000 ft (1 525 m); max vertical climb, 1,192 ft/min (6,05 m/sec); time on station (at radius of 57 mls/92 km), 3 hrs 52 min.

Weights: Empty equipped, 13,678 lb (6 204 kg); max take-off, 21,844 lb (9 908 kg).

Dimensions: Rotor diam, 53 ft 8 in (16,36 m); fuselage length, 50 ft 0¾ in (15,26 m).

Notes: Winner of the US Navy's LAMPS (Light Airborne Multi-Purpose System) Mk III helicopter contest, the SH-60B is intended to fulfil both anti-submarine warfare (ASW) and anti-ship surveillance and targeting (ASST) missions and the first of five prototypes was flown on 12 December 1979, and the last on 14 July 1980. Evolved from the UH-60A (see page 245), the SH-60B is intended to serve aboard DD-963 destroyers, DDG-47 Aegis cruisers and FFG-7 guided-missile frigates as an integral extension of the sensor and weapon system of the launching vessel. The US Navy has a requirement for 204 SH-60Bs, the first of which was delivered in October 1983, and for 195 simplified SH-60Fs without MAD gear.

SIKORSKY S-76 MK II

Country of Origin: USA.
Type: Fourteen-seat commercial transport helicopter.
Power Plant: Two 700 shp Allison 250-C30 turboshafts.
Performance: Max speed, 179 mph (288 km/h); max cruise, 167 mph (268 km/h); range cruise, 145 mph (233 km/h); hovering ceiling (in ground effect), 5,100 ft (1 524 m), (out of ground effect), 1,400 ft (427 m); range (full payload and 30 min reserve), 460 mls (740 km).
Weights: Empty 5,600 lb (2 540 kg); max take-off, 10,300 lb (4 672 kg).
Dimensions: Rotor diam, 44 ft 0 in (13,41 m); fuselage length, 43 ft 4½ in (13,22 m).
Notes: The first of four prototypes of the S-76 flew on 13 March 1977, and customer deliveries commenced 1979, with more than 220 delivered by the beginning of 1984, when a production rate was being increased from two to four monthly. The S-76 is unique among Sikorsky commercial helicopters in that conceptually it owes nothing to an existing military model, although it has been designed to conform with appropriate military specifications and military customers were included among contracts for helicopters of this type that had been ordered by the beginning of 1984. The S-76 may be fitted with extended-range tanks, cargo hook and rescue hoist. The main rotor is a scaled-down version of that used by the UH-60. All S-76s have been modified to Mk II standards.

SIKORSKY AUH-76

Country of Origin: USA.
Type: General-purpose military utility helicopter.
Power Plant: Two 700 shp Allison 250-C30S or 1,000 shp Pratt & Whitney PT6B-36 turboshafts.
Performance: (Allison 250-C30S) Max speed, 178 mph (287 km/h); average cruise, 173 mph (278 km/h); range (with 30 min reserves), 465 mls (749 km).
Weights: Empty, 5,610 lb (2 545 kg); max take-off, 10,300 lb (4 672 kg).
Dimensions: Rotor diam, 44 ft 0 in (13,41 m); fuselage length, 43 ft 5 in (13,21 m).
Notes: A derivative of the S-76 Mk II (see page 247), the AUH-76, which entered flight test early 1982 and completed weapons qualifications in August of that year, is a multi-role helicopter suitable for use as a gunship, utility transport accommodating up to 12 troops, or for scouting and reconnaissance missions. It has a high-strength fuel tank, armoured pilots' seats and sliding doors in both sides of the fuselage, a fixed undercarriage being optional. In armed configuration, it has weapons pylons and provision for door-mounted weapons. Podded 7,62-mm or 0·5-in (12,7-mm) machine guns, or 7,62-mm miniguns may be fitted to the outrigger-type pylons, optional ordnance including pods of 19 2·75-in (7,0-mm) folding-fin rockets or up to 16 TOW anti-armour missiles. Twelve H-76s were ordered by the Philippines in 1983, together with five S-76 Utility helicopters for SAR and other roles.

WESTLAND SEA KING

Country of Origin: United Kingdom (US licence).

Type: Anti-submarine warfare and search-and-rescue helicopter.

Power Plant: Two 1,660 shp Rolls-Royce Gnome H.1400-1 turboshafts.

Performance: Max speed, 143 mph (230 km/h); max continuous cruise at sea level, 131 mph (211 km/h); hovering ceiling (in ground effect), 5,000 ft (1 525 m), (out of ground effect), 3,200 ft (975 m); range (standard fuel), 764 mls (1 230 km), (auxiliary fuel), 937 mls (1 507 km).

Weights: Empty equipped (ASW), 13,672 lb (6 201 kg), (SAR), 12,376 lb (5 613 kg); max take-off, 21,000 lb (9 525 kg).

Dimensions: Rotor diam, 62 ft 0 in (18,90 m); fuselage length, 55 ft 9¾ in (17,01 m).

Notes: The Sea King Mk 2 is an uprated version of the basic ASW and SAR derivative of the licence-built S-61 D (see 1982 edition), the first Mk 2 being flown on 30 June 1974, and being one of 10 Sea King Mk 50s ordered by the Australian Navy. Twenty-one to the Royal Navy as HAS Mk 2s, and 15 examples of a SAR version to the RAF as HAR Mk 3s. Current production version is the HAS Mk 5, delivery of 17 to Royal Navy having commenced October 1980, and a further eight being ordered in 1983. All HAS Mk 2s being brought up to Mk 5 standards and five fitted with Thorn-EMI searchwater radar (as illustrated) for airborne early warning duty.

WESTLAND COMMANDO

Country of Origin: United Kingdom (US licence).
Type: Tactical transport helicopter.
Power Plant: Two 1,590 shp Rolls-Royce Gnome H-1400-1 turboshafts.
Performance: (Mk 2 at 21,000 lb/9 526 kg) Max speed, 140 mph (225 km/h) at sea level; normal operating speed, 129 mph (207 km/h) at sea level; initial inclined climb, 2,020 ft/ min (10,3 m/sec); hovering ceiling (in ground effect), 5,000 ft (1 525 m), (out of ground effect), 3,200 ft (975 m); range (with max. payload), 276 mls (445 km).
Weights: Basic equipped, 11,174 lb (5 069 kg); max take-off, 21,000 lb (9 526 kg).
Dimensions: Rotor diam, 62 ft 0 in (18,90 m); fuselage length, 55 ft 9¾ in (17,01 m).
Notes: The Commando is a Westland-developed land-based army support helicopter derivative of the Sea King (see page 249), the interim Mk 1 having minimum changes from the ASW helicopter. The first of five Mk 1s was flown on 12 September 1973, subsequent examples being built to Mk 2 standard with the uprated Gnome turboshafts selected for the Sea King Mk 50. The five Mk 1s and 23 Mk 2s were supplied to Egypt and four Mk 2s to Qatar, and 15 similar helicopters were supplied (as Sea King HC Mk 4s—illustrated) to the Royal Navy commando squadrons. In mid-1982, it was announced that a further eight were to be ordered. The Mk 3 (with sponsons and retractable undercarriage) flew on 14 June 1982, eight having been ordered by Qatar.

WESTLAND WG 13 LYNX

Country of Origin: United Kingdom.
Type: Multi-purpose, ASW and transport helicopter.
Power Plant: Two 900 shp Rolls-Royce BS. 360-07-26 Gem 100 turboshafts.
Performance: Max speed, 207 mph (333 km/h); max. continuous sea level cruise, 170 mph (273 km/h); max inclined climb, 1,174 ft/min (11,05 m/sec); hovering ceiling (out of ground effect), 12,000 ft (3 660 m); max range (internal fuel), 391 mls (629 km); max ferry range, 787 mls (1 266 km).
Weights: (HAS Mk 2) Operational empty, 6,767–6,999 lb (3 069–3 179 kg); max take-off, 9,500 lb (4 309 kg).
Dimensions: Rotor diam, 42 ft 0 in (12,80 m); fuselage length, 39 ft 1¼ in (11,92 m).
Notes: The first of 13 development Lynxes was flown on 21 March 1971, with the first production example (an HAS Mk 2) flying on 10 February 1976. By the beginning of 1984 a total of 312 was on order, including 40 for the French Navy, 83 for the Royal Navy, 114 for the British Army, two for the Argentine Navy, eight for the Danish Navy, 12 for the German Navy, nine for the Brazilian Navy, six for Norway, 24 for the Netherlands Navy, three for the Nigerian Navy and three of a general-purpose version for Qatar. The Lynx AH MK 1 is the British Army's general utility version and the Lynx HAS Mk 2 is the ASW version for the Royal Navy. Eighteen of the Dutch and 14 of the French Lynx have uprated engines. Last two British Army Lynx to be completed to partial Lynx 3 standard with uprated Gem 41s.

WESTLAND 30-100

Country of Origin: United Kingdom.

Type: Transport and utility helicopter.

Power Plant: Two 1,265 shp Rolls-Royce Gem 60-1 turbo-shafts.

Performance: Max speed (at 10,500 lb/4 763 kg), 163 mph (263 km/h) at 3,000 ft (915 m); hovering ceiling (in ground effect), 7,200 ft (2 195 m), (out of ground effect), 5,000 ft (1 525 m); range (seven passengers), 426 mls (686 km).

Weights: Operational empty (typical), 6,880 lb (3 120 kg); max take-off, 12,800 lb (5 806 kg).

Dimensions: Rotor diam, 43 ft 8 in (13,31 m); fuselage length, 47 ft 0 in (14,33 m).

Notes: The WG 30, flown for the first time on 10 April 1979, is a private venture development of the Lynx (see page 251) featuring an entirely new fuselage offering a substantial increase in capacity. Aimed primarily at the multi-role military helicopter field, the WG 30 has a crew of two and in the transport role can carry 17–22 passengers. Commitment to the WG 30 at the time of closing for press covers initial production of 41, deliveries of which began January 1982. British Airways has purchased two and four have been supplied to the US-based Airspur Airline, other US purchasers including SFO Helicopter Airlines and Helicopter Hire. The WG 30 utilises more than 85% of the proven systems of the WG 13 Lynx, and the WG 30-200 (flown on 3 September 1983) differs from the -100 in having General Electric CT7-2 turboshafts.

INDEX OF AIRCRAFT TYPES